Language Arts Trivial Pursuit

Junior High Level

by
Mary Anne McElmurry, O.P.
Kino Learning Center, Inc.

Cover by Tom Sjoerdsma

Copyright © Good Apple, 1992

ISBN No. 0-86653-650-7

Printing No. 987654321

Good Apple
1204 Buchanan St., Box 299
Carthage, IL 62321-0299

SIMON & SCHUSTER *A Paramount Communications Company*

Description of Kino Learning Center

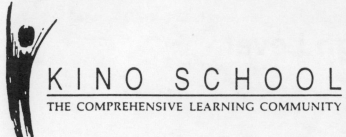

KINO SCHOOL
THE COMPREHENSIVE LEARNING COMMUNITY

Kino Learning Center, Inc., is a private, non-profit elementary and secondary school founded in Tucson, Arizona, in 1975 by parents seeking a futuristic learning model for children. The school not only emphasizes the conventional skills of reading, writing and computing, but goes beyond these basics to the contemporary skills of choosing, relating, valuing, creating and learning how to learn.

Within the prepared environment of the school, each student is free to choose from worthwhile options, a sequence of activities unique to his/her needs and experiences, and in which he/she finds success, interest and pleasure. Each student is free to develop in the way and at the pace appropriate to his/her needs, abilities and interests. The school places special emphasis on individual discovery, on firsthand experience and on creative work.

At Kino Learning Center, Inc., adults, teenagers and children mutually engaged in the learning process are continually in the process of changing and growing, for to learn is to change. And to experience joy in learning is to delight in life itself, for learning and life are one.

The curriculum at Kino Learning Center, Inc., consists of teacher-made learning packets containing facts, processes and values related to topics of interest to the students. These learning packets have been expanded into workbooks for use by teachers and students throughout the United States and Europe. Over forty books are presently in circulation. The profits from the sale of these books are used to enhance the learning environment at Kino Learning Center, Inc.

For more information about Kino Learning Center, Inc., write 6625 N. First Ave., Tucson, AZ 85718 or call (602) 297-7278.

To the Teacher

Following is a list of the books used as references in writing the mythology questions.

Mythology

Mighty Myth, Greta Barclay Lipson and Sidney M. Bolkosky, Ph.D.
Mythology Archeology–Architecture, Diane Sylvester and Mary Wiemann
Greek Mythology for Everyone, Donald Richardson
Gods, Men and Monsters from the Greek Myths, Michael Gibson
Favorite Greek Myths, Mary Pope Osborne
Greek Gods and Heroes, Alice Law
Greek Mythology, John Pinsent

GA1384

Purpose of Game

The purpose of *Language Arts Trivial Pursuit* is to have fun and enjoy language arts while learning and reinforcing language arts in the following categories:

Books and Authors

Mythology

Literacy Terms

Skill Builders

Game Parts

Gameboard

Carefully remove and unfold the gameboard from the center of the book.

Playing Cards

Language Arts Trivial Pursuit contains 232 game cards with four questions and answers per card. Each page of the book contains eight game cards. Separate the cards by cutting along the solid lines. To assure greater durability, you may want to laminate each page before cutting out the cards.

Die

One die is needed to play *Language Arts Trivial Pursuit.* A pattern for making a die is shown at the right. Glue the pattern to a piece of tagboard. Cut out the pattern. Fold along the solid lines. Place glue on the dotted tabs. Fold the tabs inside the cube. Hold until dry. (Note: You may want to obtain a commercially made die from a toy store.)

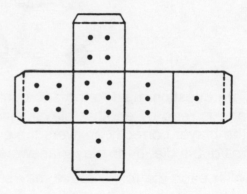

Pawns

You will need a game pawn for each player or team. Buttons, coins, bottle caps or other similar items may be used. Pawns may also be purchased at a toy store.

Container

Place the game cards in a small box for safekeeping. Store your gameboard, playing cards, die and pawns in a box or Baggie.

GA1384

Rules for Play

1. Each player selects a pawn and writes his/her name on the Game Tally Sheet.

2. Each player rolls the die. The player rolling the highest number begins the game. In a tie, these players roll again to determine who begins the game.

3. The first player rolls the die again. Starting from the hub in the center of the board, the player moves the pawn the indicated number of spaces along any spoke. The first move for each player will end either in a category headquarters at the end of a spoke or in a category space.

4. When a pawn lands in a category space or category headquarters, the player is asked a question in that category.

Category Spaces and Headquarters Are Indicated by Geometric Shapes as Follows:

● Books and Authors

■ Mythology

▲ Literacy Terms

⬡ Skill Builders

5. The question, next to the appropriate geometric shape, is taken from the card box and is read by another player. Answers are on the opposite side of each card. If the player correctly answers the question, the player's turn continues with another roll of the die. If the player answers incorrectly, the turn passes to the left.

6. With each die roll, a move may be made in either direction around the octagonal path or on any of the spoke paths. A combination move along the octagonal path and up a spoke path is permitted. Backtracking—a combination of forward and backward moves on one die roll—is not permitted. For example, if a player's pawn is one space from a desired category space or headquarters and a die roll of five is made, a move of three forward and two backward cannot be made.

7. A player must always move the number of spaces shown on the die.

8. The card is placed at the end of the pile after each question.

9. When a player has correctly answered a question in a category headquarters at the end of a spoke along the octagonal path, a check mark is placed by the player's name under the appropriate geometric shape on the Game Tally Sheet. If the player answers incorrectly, the pawn must leave the headquarters on the next turn. It can later reenter headquarters, and the player may attempt another question for credit.

10. A player landing on one of the four "Roll Again" spaces continues his/her turn by rolling the die again.

11. A player landing on "Player May Choose" may select to answer a question for any of the four categories during his/her turn.

12. Any number of pawns may occupy the same space at the same time.

13. When a pawn lands in the hub, before the player has met the four headquarter requirements to be able to win the game, the hub is treated as a wild card space and the player chooses the category for the subsequent question.

14. After a player has correctly answered a question in all four category headquarters, the player's pawn must make its way to the hub to attempt to win the game.

15. The pawn must land in the hub by an exact roll of the die. If a player overshoots the hub, he/she must successfully answer a question in the category on which he/she lands and try again to enter the hub on an exact roll of the die. If the question is not answered correctly, the player must wait for his/her next turn.

16. When the pawn lands in the hub, opposing players select the category for a final question by simple agreement or a vote, and the next card is drawn.

17. If the question is answered correctly, the game is won. If the question is answered incorrectly, the player must leave the hub on the next turn and reenter for another question.

18. Because a correct answer always means another roll of the die, a player may meet the game-winning requirements on the first turn. If this happens, any player who has not yet had a turn is permitted a chance to duplicate the feat and create a tie.

19. The players determine how long they have to answer a question and how precise an answer must be. Time and accuracy may vary for each player.

Tally Sheets

Make copies of the tally sheets below. Put a check (√) in the box when you or your team lands on a headquarter space and correctly answers the question for that category.

Game Tally Sheet					
Player or Team	●	■	▲	⬡	The Win!

Game Tally Sheet					
Player or Team	●	■	▲	⬡	The Win!

GA1382

● This author wrote *The Black Cauldron*, where an army of warriors is made from stolen bodies of the slain.

■ She is the Greek queen of the gods and goddesses.

▲ A division in a poem consisting of a group of related lines

⬡ Complete the word with the letters *e* and *i* in the correct order: REL __?__ F.

● Milo, an American schoolboy who regarded the process of seeking knowledge as the greatest waste of time, is found in this book.

■ The Romans prayed to her for wisdom.

▲ This is a principal opponent or the main character in a story.

⬡ Add the suffix *ly* to the word *complete*.

● He wrote and illustrated *The Little Cocherel*.

■ She is the Roman queen of the gods and goddesses.

▲ The pattern in which accented and unaccented syllables are repeated in each line of a poem.

⬡ Add the suffix *ous* to the word *fame*.

● This is a very popular Canadian novel by L.M. Montgomery. In this story, an elderly brother and sister send for a boy from an orphanage to help them on their farm and end up with a girl.

■ He is the Greek god who rules the ocean.

▲ The implied attitude of a writer toward the subject about which he or she is writing

⬡ What is the adjective in the following sentence: Joe volunteered for the dirty job?

● She is the author of *The Summer of the Swans*. This is about Sara, Aunt Willie and the disappearance of Sara's brother Charlie.

■ This god has the same name in both Greek and Roman mythology.

▲ A division of a play in which there is a change in time or place

⬡ Choose the correct word for the following sentence: I never (loose, lose) a trivia contest.

● This American artist illustrated *Little Lord Fauntleroy*.

■ The Roman goddess to whom you would pray for physical beauty

▲ A stage convention which allows an actor to express his/her inner thoughts in a speech

⬡ Choose the correct synonym for *fragrance*. (exotic, aroma, hardy)

● She is the author of *The Secret Garden*.

■ He is the Greek god of the messengers.

▲ The turning point in a story or play

⬡ Choose the correct word. Yes, this is (he, him).

● This is a popular writer of American teenage fiction. One of her more well-known books is *Forever*.

■ He is the Greek god who rules success in war.

▲ A comparison using the words *like* or *as*

⬡ What is the verb that *slowly* modifies? The old car slowly chugged forward.

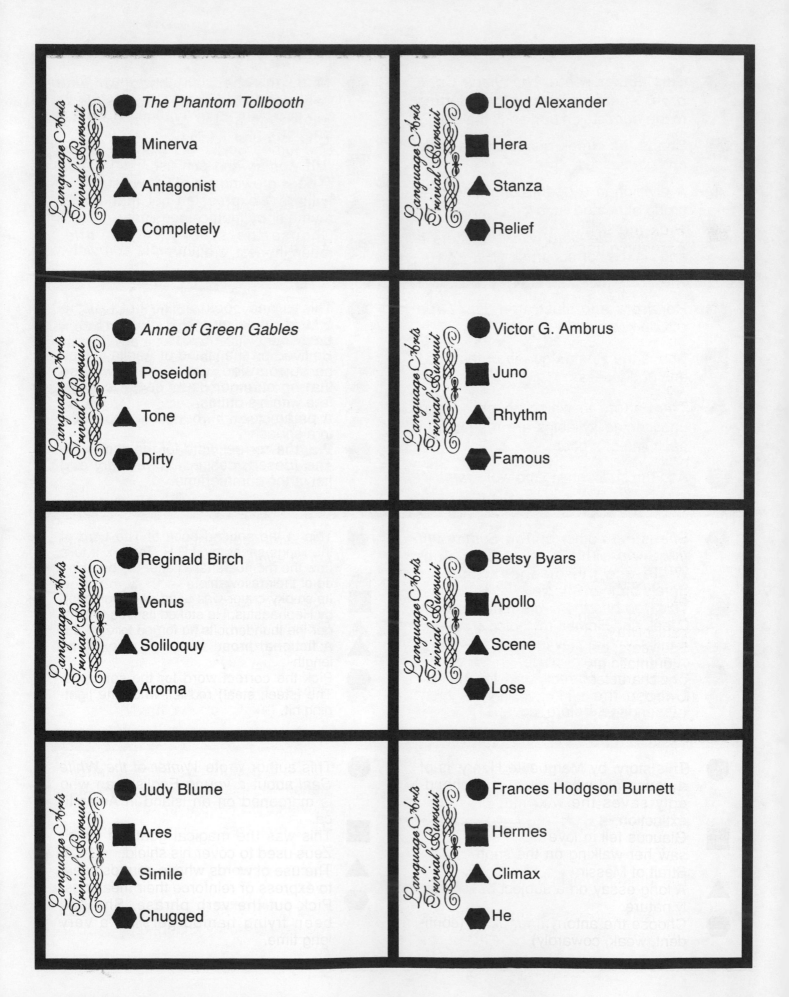

Language Arts Trivial Pursuit

- ● *The Phantom Tollbooth*
- ■ Minerva
- ▲ Antagonist
- ⬡ Completely

Language Arts Trivial Pursuit

- ● Lloyd Alexander
- ■ Hera
- ▲ Stanza
- ⬡ Relief

Language Arts Trivial Pursuit

- ● *Anne of Green Gables*
- ■ Poseidon
- ▲ Tone
- ⬡ Dirty

Language Arts Trivial Pursuit

- ● Victor G. Ambrus
- ■ Juno
- ▲ Rhythm
- ⬡ Famous

Language Arts Trivial Pursuit

- ● Reginald Birch
- ■ Venus
- ▲ Soliloquy
- ⬡ Aroma

Language Arts Trivial Pursuit

- ● Betsy Byars
- ■ Apollo
- ▲ Scene
- ⬡ Lose

Language Arts Trivial Pursuit

- ● Judy Blume
- ■ Ares
- ▲ Simile
- ⬡ Chugged

Language Arts Trivial Pursuit

- ● Frances Hodgson Burnett
- ■ Hermes
- ▲ Climax
- ⬡ He

GA1384

● This author wrote *Walt Disney: an American Original* about the rags-to-riches story of the famous cartoonist.

■ She is the Greek goddess of the hunt.

▲ A play having a serious mood and ending in death or disaster

⬡ Identify the three prepositions in this sentence: In spite of the monsoon, we went with them.

● This author wrote *Ellis Island and Other Stories*. It is a four-part novella about the adventures of the immigrant at the turn of the century.

■ What was the first race of mythological giants called?

▲ The portion of a story or play that follows the climax

⬡ Select the misspelled word and correct it. (legislasure, thesaurus, veteran)

● This author wrote *Judy Blume's Story*. This is a biography about the famous author.

■ Who is the Greek king of the gods?

▲ A line or phrase repeated at regular points in a poem, usually at the end of each stanza

⬡ Choose the correct analogy for these words, *cold:hot*. (high:low; kind:indulgent; fast:quick)

● This author wrote *Death Be Not Proud*, a true story of his brave son who was dying of a brain tumor.

■ In order to keep order in his world, where did Uranus keep his children imprisoned?

▲ A story about superhuman beings—gods, goddesses or heroes

⬡ Choose the correct spelling of the following word: grammar, grammer, grammor.

● This author wrote *Freedom Train: the Story of Harriet Tubman*.

■ In Greek mythology, who was Father Sky?

▲ A play on words involving two words that sound alike or a word that has two different meanings

⬡ Choose the correct meaning of the word *hypothesis* as it is used in the following sentence: My hypothesis is that Henry took the money. (mistake, theory, act)

● This small boy is found in stories by H. E. Todd. Strange and magical things happen to him.

■ Who plotted to overthrow Uranus?

▲ A person who tells a story or poem

⬡ Choose the correct form of *who*. (Who, Whom) is on the phone?

⬡ Kyro Petrovshoya Wayne wrote this true story about a family and their Doberman.

■ In Greek mythology, who was Mother Earth?

▲ The repetition of words or syllables with similar sounds

⬡ Choose the word or phrase that is closest in meaning to the word *dubious*. (hopeful, favorable, doubtful)

● He is an American folk hero, in reality William F. Cody, a rider for the Pony Express and frontier scout during the Civil War.

■ With what did Kronos wound his father?

▲ The rate at which a story moves, its beat or rhythm

⬡ Choose the correct spelling of the following word: tommorow, tomorow, tomorrow.

GA1384

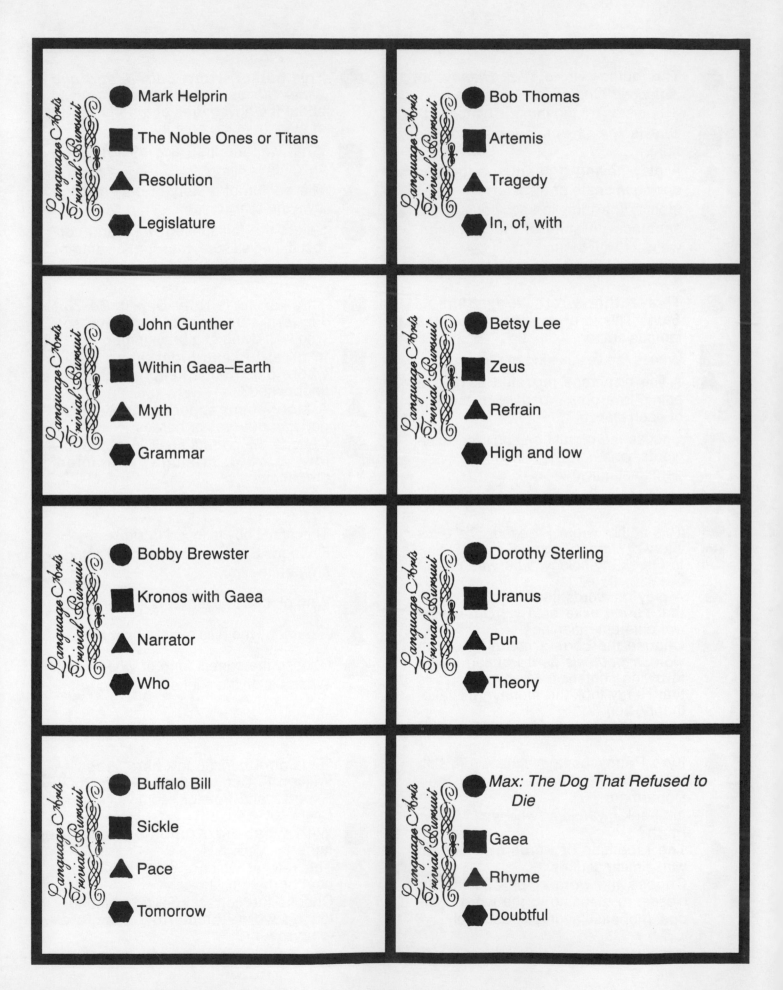

Language Arts Trivial Pursuit

● Mark Helprin

■ The Noble Ones or Titans

▲ Resolution

⬡ Legislature

Language Arts Trivial Pursuit

● Bob Thomas

■ Artemis

▲ Tragedy

⬡ In, of, with

Language Arts Trivial Pursuit

● John Gunther

■ Within Gaea–Earth

▲ Myth

⬡ Grammar

Language Arts Trivial Pursuit

● Betsy Lee

■ Zeus

▲ Refrain

⬡ High and low

Language Arts Trivial Pursuit

● Bobby Brewster

■ Kronos with Gaea

▲ Narrator

⬡ Who

Language Arts Trivial Pursuit

● Dorothy Sterling

■ Uranus

▲ Pun

⬡ Theory

Language Arts Trivial Pursuit

● Buffalo Bill

■ Sickle

▲ Pace

⬡ Tomorrow

Language Arts Trivial Pursuit

● *Max: The Dog That Refused to Die*

■ Gaea

▲ Rhyme

⬡ Doubtful

GA1384

● This novel by Rudyard Kipling tells of the spoiled adolescent son of an American millionaire who has to earn his keep on a fishing boat for the summer.

■ Uranus' blood mixed with the waves from the sea produced the goddess of love. Who was this?

▲ A contrast between the way things seem to be and the way they actually are

⬡ Choose the correct spelling of the following word: hapened, happened, happed.

● This literary character was given the opportunity to carry an untainted knowledge of the past into the future but chose to exist as before.

■ Rhea hid this last son in a cave on the island of Crete.

▲ An opening section or scene that serves as an introduction to a work of literature or a play

⬡ Pick the antonym for *partial*. (unreal, partly, entire)

● He is the author of *The Canterbury Tales*.

■ What were the last three goddesses born of Uranus and Gaea called?

▲ A form of verse designed specifically to be amusing

⬡ Identify all the nouns in the following sentence: Fruits and sandwiches are examples of this type of food.

● This author wrote the classic *The Virginian*.

■ What were Zeus and his brothers and sisters collectively called?

▲ Person through whose eyes a reader sees what happens in a story

⬡ Pick the synonym for *mimic*. (display, open, imitate)

● She is the author of the Henry Huggins and Ramona books. *Fifteen* is among the more popular of her selections.

■ Which Greek god swallowed each of his children as they were born to his wife Rhea?

▲ A suggested or implied comparison between two things

⬡ Identify the appositive in this sentence: My white and black cat, Spat, has four black paws.

● This author wrote a series of books about the Wilder family, one of which was *Little House on the Prairie*.

■ With whom did Zeus fall in love?

▲ Words that rhyme within the same line of a poem

⬡ Identify the suffix of this word: *acquaintance*.

● He was generally regarded as the most brilliant English book illustrator of his period (1792-1878). He was Dickens' first illustrator, providing pictures for *Oliver Twist*.

■ Who was Kronos and Rhea's last son?

▲ Giving human characteristics to something that is not human

⬡ Identify the direct object in this sentence: Snakes shed their skins at regular intervals.

● This story, written by Marietta Moshen, is about a young girl who spent four years in a Nazi concentration camp.

■ Who did Zeus swallow along with Metis?

▲ An obvious and extravagant exaggeration not meant to be taken literally

⬡ Pick the correct spelling of this word: becuase, because, becuse.

GA1384

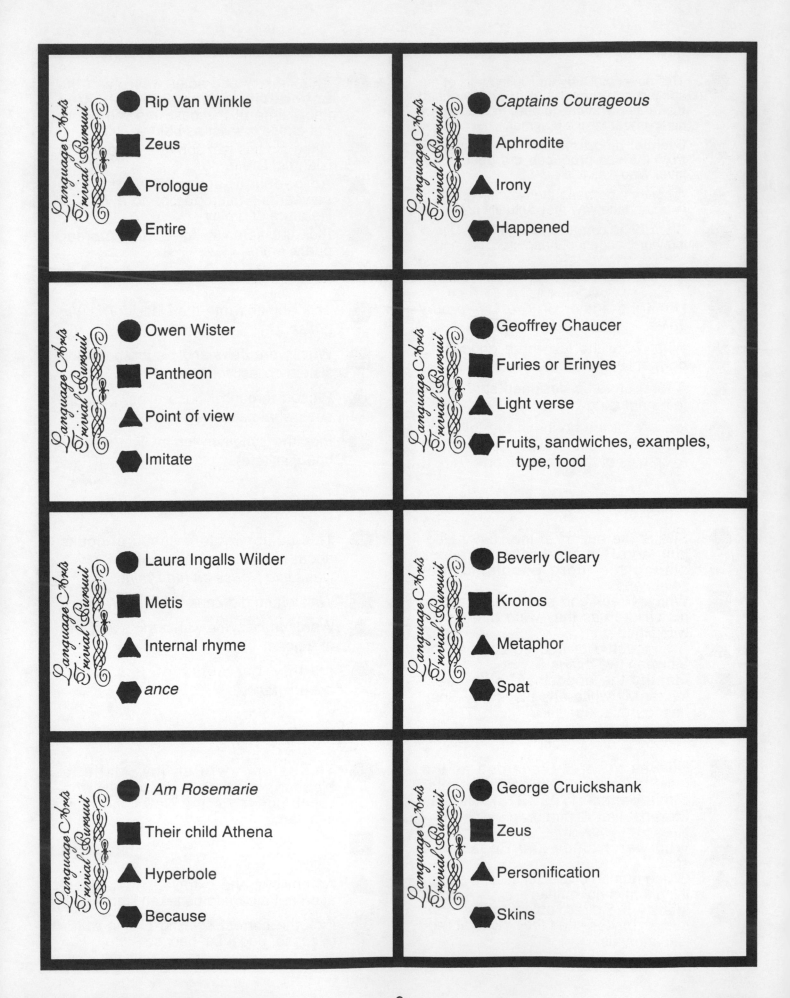

Card 1 (top left)

Language Arts Trivial Pursuit

- ● Rip Van Winkle
- ■ Zeus
- ▲ Prologue
- ⬡ Entire

Card 2 (top right)

Language Arts Trivial Pursuit

- ● *Captains Courageous*
- ■ Aphrodite
- ▲ Irony
- ⬡ Happened

Card 3 (middle-upper left)

Language Arts Trivial Pursuit

- ● Owen Wister
- ■ Pantheon
- ▲ Point of view
- ⬡ Imitate

Card 4 (middle-upper right)

Language Arts Trivial Pursuit

- ● Geoffrey Chaucer
- ■ Furies or Erinyes
- ▲ Light verse
- ⬡ Fruits, sandwiches, examples, type, food

Card 5 (middle-lower left)

Language Arts Trivial Pursuit

- ● Laura Ingalls Wilder
- ■ Metis
- ▲ Internal rhyme
- ⬡ *ance*

Card 6 (middle-lower right)

Language Arts Trivial Pursuit

- ● Beverly Cleary
- ■ Kronos
- ▲ Metaphor
- ⬡ Spat

Card 7 (bottom left)

Language Arts Trivial Pursuit

- ● *I Am Rosemarie*
- ■ Their child Athena
- ▲ Hyperbole
- ⬡ Because

Card 8 (bottom right)

Language Arts Trivial Pursuit

- ● George Cruickshank
- ■ Zeus
- ▲ Personification
- ⬡ Skins

GA1384

● This story by Farley Mowat is a true story of a man who spent time in the Canadian wilderness with a family of wolves. The book was made into a movie.

■ Who freed Athena by splitting Zeus' skull on an anvil with one blow from his silver ax?

▲ A short work of nonfiction that explores a particular topic

⬡ Pick the correct form of *who*. (Who, Whom) did you pay for the candy?

● This author wrote *A Farewell to Arms*, the poignant love story of an English nurse and an American ambulance lieutenant during the war.

■ Which daughter of Zeus was known as The Apportioner who twists the threads which make a life strong or weak?

▲ The repetition of initial consonant sounds of two or more words that are close together

⬡ Find the gerund in this sentence: Do you like skiing?

● This true story written by Richard E. Peck is about two brothers, John Cappelletti and Joey, who is a leukemia victim.

■ From what terrible prophecy did Zeus escape by giving birth to Athena from his head?

▲ A word or expression not meant literally

⬡ Choose the correct antonym for *elaborate*. (vogue, simple, complicated)

● He was the creator of animated cartoons and produced the first of his Mickey Mouse series in 1928.

■ Which daughter of Zeus was known as The Inflexible who cuts the thread which measures the length of life?

▲ The use of a pleasant, harmonious-sounding combination of words, generally in poetry

⬡ Choose the word that means "a strong feeling of dislike." (pacify, parasite, repugnance)

● This book, written by Sansan, is the true story of a girl who escaped from China.

■ Who was Zeus' favorite child?

▲ A sudden shift backward in time

⬡ Pick the correct synonym for *residual*. (permanent, remaining, whole)

● This writer and novelist created the popular Peter Pan and companions.

■ Which daughter of Zeus was known as The Spinner who spins the thread of life with light and dark lines which stand for degrees of happiness and sadness?

▲ The character about whom the reader or audience is most concerned

⬡ Identify the prepositional phrase. Driving within the speed limit saves lives.

● Ichabod Crane was the unfortunate character in this story.

■ Clotho, Atropos and Lachesis, the three daughters of Zeus and Thenius, were known as the __?__.

▲ A work of literature designed to be performed by actors in front of an audience

⬡ Identify the verbs in this sentence: The rock group played and danced to their song.

● This author wrote nearly 130 popular books for boys, all based on the idea that a struggle against poverty and temptation usually leads a boy to fame and wealth.

■ Which daughter of Zeus had super intelligence because she was born from the brain of Zeus?

▲ A mental picture or impression that appeals to one of the senses

⬡ Choose the correct spelling of the following word: arrogent, arrogant, arogant.

GA1384

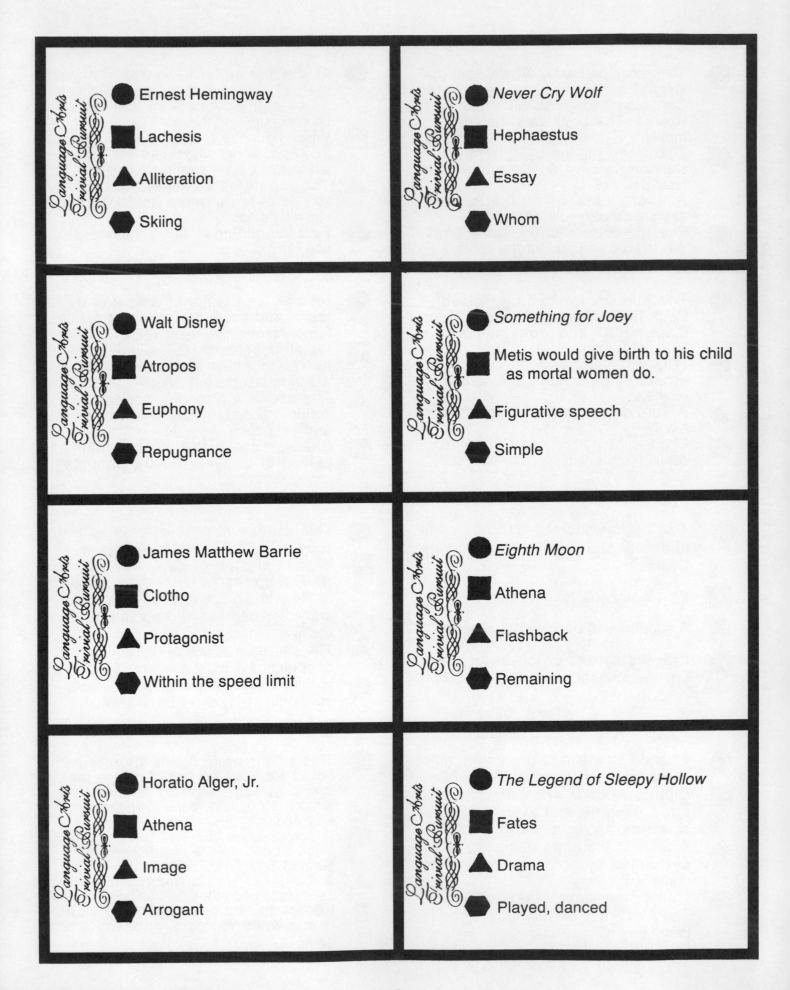

Language Arts Trivial Pursuit

- ● Ernest Hemingway
- ■ Lachesis
- ▲ Alliteration
- ⬡ Skiing

Language Arts Trivial Pursuit

- ● *Never Cry Wolf*
- ■ Hephaestus
- ▲ Essay
- ⬡ Whom

Language Arts Trivial Pursuit

- ● Walt Disney
- ■ Atropos
- ▲ Euphony
- ⬡ Repugnance

Language Arts Trivial Pursuit

- ● *Something for Joey*
- ■ Metis would give birth to his child as mortal women do.
- ▲ Figurative speech
- ⬡ Simple

Language Arts Trivial Pursuit

- ● James Matthew Barrie
- ■ Clotho
- ▲ Protagonist
- ⬡ Within the speed limit

Language Arts Trivial Pursuit

- ● *Eighth Moon*
- ■ Athena
- ▲ Flashback
- ⬡ Remaining

Language Arts Trivial Pursuit

- ● Horatio Alger, Jr.
- ■ Athena
- ▲ Image
- ⬡ Arrogant

Language Arts Trivial Pursuit

- ● *The Legend of Sleepy Hollow*
- ■ Fates
- ▲ Drama
- ⬡ Played, danced

GA1384

● Frank L. Baum wrote fantasies for children about the Land of Oz. This book was the first.

■ Why did Athena hate Aphrodite?

▲ A humorous five-line poem

⬡ Pick out the adjective in this sentence: The lunch tasted yummy.

● This author wrote *Gentle Ben*, about a friendship between a boy and an Alaskan bear.

■ Who is the Greek god of the underworld?

▲ A clue or hint in a story or play that gives the reader some indication of what will eventually happen

⬡ Pick out the adjective in this sentence: That star was made for you.

● This novel by Robert Cornier is set in a private, Catholic boys' day school with Brother Leon being in charge.

■ What was the contest between Athena and Arachne?

▲ A three-line poem that describes a single image

⬡ The protagonist of the story is the (main character, author, villain).

● This book, by Peter Dickinson, is about a group of children who fake an appearance of a monster in a Scottish loch.

■ Who guarded the gates of Tartarus in the underworld?

▲ The second line is run-on and requires the first line of the succeeding couplet to complete its meaning

⬡ Choose the synonym for *retrospect*. (expected, confident, looking back)

● This author wrote *King of the Wind*, about an Arabian horse's travels to England.

■ What did Arachne do when she lost the contest of tapestries to Athena?

▲ Poetry that has no regular sequence or pattern or rhythm

⬡ Name the direct object in this sentence: Members of the spider family have eight legs.

● This author wrote *A Tree Grows in Brooklyn*, about a girl growing up in Brooklyn before World War I.

■ After obtaining permission from Zeus to marry Persephone, Hades abducted her by disguising himself as a _?_.

▲ Metaphor in which the suggested resemblance of the things compared is in some respect so false as to be cancelled out

⬡ Pick out all of the pronouns in this sentence: She nursed him back to health, and he was indebted to her for life.

● The first true detective story is generally held to be this popular tale by Edgar Allan Poe.

■ To what form did Athena change Arachne's body?

▲ The exact dictionary meaning of a word

⬡ To make restitution is (reparation, cover up, making money).

● This author wrote the well-known book *The Little Prince*, about a prince who visits Earth from his own planet.

■ Which god was allowed to create man?

▲ A poem or stanza of eight lines

⬡ Pick the synonym for *mischievous*. (imitate, playful, score)

9

GA1384

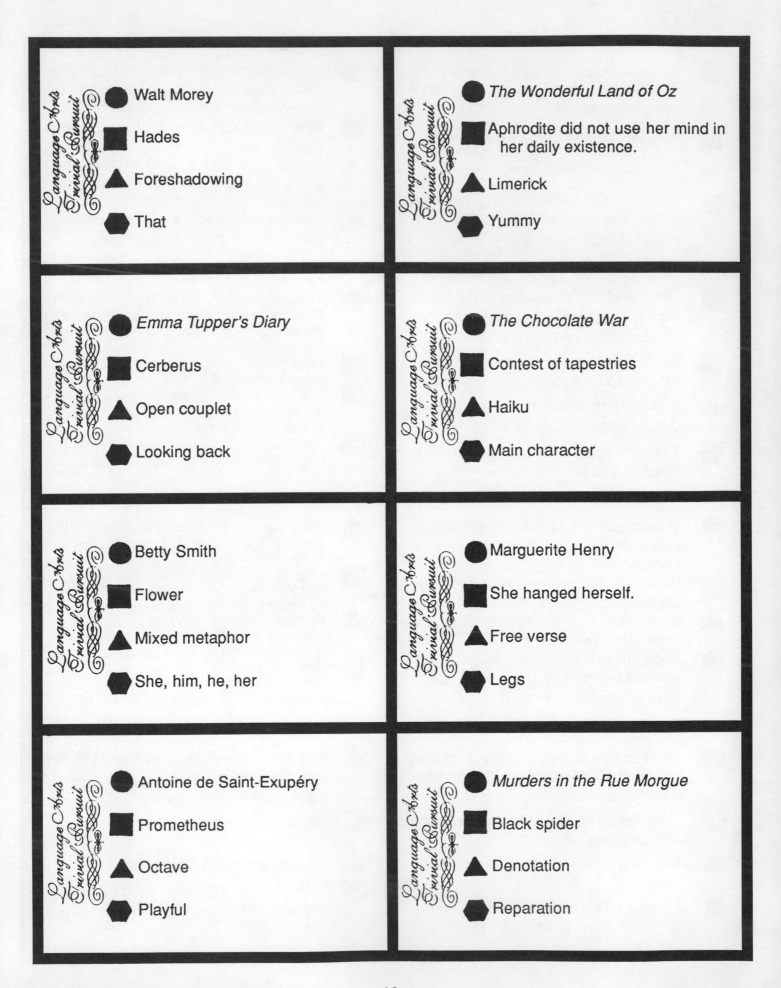

Language Arts Trivial Pursuit

- ● Walt Morey
- ■ Hades
- ▲ Foreshadowing
- ⬡ That

Language Arts Trivial Pursuit

- ● *The Wonderful Land of Oz*
- ■ Aphrodite did not use her mind in her daily existence.
- ▲ Limerick
- ⬡ Yummy

Language Arts Trivial Pursuit

- ● *Emma Tupper's Diary*
- ■ Cerberus
- ▲ Open couplet
- ⬡ Looking back

Language Arts Trivial Pursuit

- ● *The Chocolate War*
- ■ Contest of tapestries
- ▲ Haiku
- ⬡ Main character

Language Arts Trivial Pursuit

- ● Betty Smith
- ■ Flower
- ▲ Mixed metaphor
- ⬡ She, him, he, her

Language Arts Trivial Pursuit

- ● Marguerite Henry
- ■ She hanged herself.
- ▲ Free verse
- ⬡ Legs

Language Arts Trivial Pursuit

- ● Antoine de Saint-Exupéry
- ■ Prometheus
- ▲ Octave
- ⬡ Playful

Language Arts Trivial Pursuit

- ● *Murders in the Rue Morgue*
- ■ Black spider
- ▲ Denotation
- ⬡ Reparation

● He wrote and illustrated the Doctor Doolittle stories.

■ Prometheus created man by mixing water and _?_.

▲ The joining of contradictory terms so as to make an expression more pointed

⬡ Identify the prepositions in this sentence: The expectant father paced up and down the hall.

● This Australian author was one of the earliest writers to make children aware of the lives of aborigines. Her best-known book is *The Way of the Whirlwind*.

■ Who was the first mortal woman created by the gods?

▲ A detailed analysis of the metrical pattern of lines and stanzas

⬡ Identify all of the adjectives in this sentence: A dry forest may burn for many weeks.

● This author wrote *The Upstairs Room*, about two Jewish girls who are hidden by a Christian family in Holland during World War II.

■ Prometheus changed the quality of men's lives by giving them the gift of _?_.

▲ A maker, in its first sense, who works with words

⬡ Pick the antonym for *imaginary*. (real, unreal, restless)

● This author wrote several stories about life in Tennessee in the mid 1800's. One such book was *Lone Hunt*.

■ What does *Pandora* mean?

▲ The stress placed on a particular syllable of a word

⬡ Select all the verbs in this sentence: The dog dug a deep hole and buried his bone.

● An American author and illustrator who created a number of eccentric children's books. He is best known for *The Twenty-One Balloons*.

■ Prometheus was punished by Zeus for giving fire to man by being chained to a great _?_.

▲ A measure in poetry consisting of two short syllables

⬡ Identify the pronouns in this sentence: A seat on the bus was saved for each of us.

● She wrote this story about the poor and fatherless Pepper children, *Five Little Peppers and How They Grew*.

■ What did Pandora have that she could not control?

▲ The comparison of the likeness of one thing to another

⬡ Pick the correct spelling of the following word: apparent, appairent, apperant.

● This author wrote *All Quiet on the Western Front*, about a German soldier during World War II.

■ Who released Prometheus from her chains?

▲ To make known

⬡ Pick the correct spelling of the following word: ambivalence, ambivalance, ambivelence.

● A book written by William Golding, about a group of boys surviving on an island without an adult

■ When Pandora was presented with the gift of a box, she was told never to _?_ it.

▲ A very old story that reflects the life of the people of a particular region

⬡ Identify the indirect object in this sentence: We played Mother the new song.

GA1384

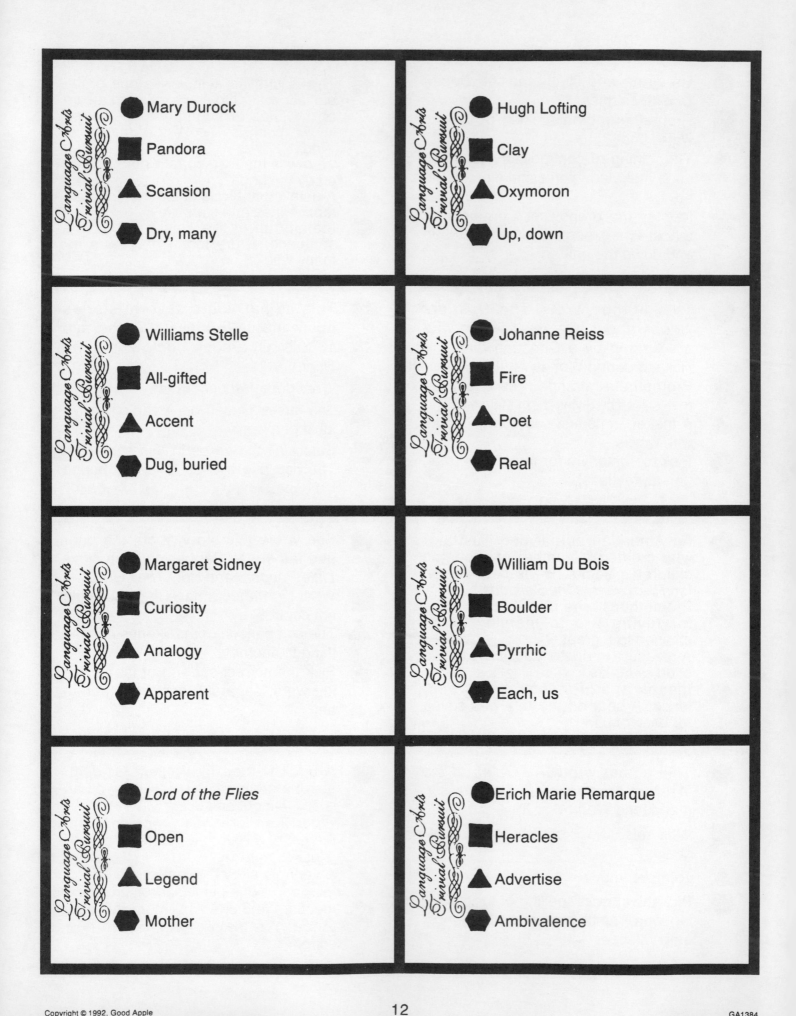

Card 1 (Language Arts Trivial Pursuit)
- ● Mary Durock
- ■ Pandora
- ▲ Scansion
- ⬡ Dry, many

Card 2 (Language Arts Trivial Pursuit)
- ● Hugh Lofting
- ■ Clay
- ▲ Oxymoron
- ⬡ Up, down

Card 3 (Language Arts Trivial Pursuit)
- ● Williams Stelle
- ■ All-gifted
- ▲ Accent
- ⬡ Dug, buried

Card 4 (Language Arts Trivial Pursuit)
- ● Johanne Reiss
- ■ Fire
- ▲ Poet
- ⬡ Real

Card 5 (Language Arts Trivial Pursuit)
- ● Margaret Sidney
- ■ Curiosity
- ▲ Analogy
- ⬡ Apparent

Card 6 (Language Arts Trivial Pursuit)
- ● William Du Bois
- ■ Boulder
- ▲ Pyrrhic
- ⬡ Each, us

Card 7 (Language Arts Trivial Pursuit)
- ● *Lord of the Flies*
- ■ Open
- ▲ Legend
- ⬡ Mother

Card 8 (Language Arts Trivial Pursuit)
- ● Erich Marie Remarque
- ■ Heracles
- ▲ Advertise
- ⬡ Ambivalence

GA1384

● Two young cousins are held prisoner in a lonely estate by a mean governess in this story written by Joan Achen.

■ What was in Pandora's box when she opened it?

▲ A story in which the personality, ability and deeds of the main character are exaggerated to the point of impossibility

⬡ Pick the synonym for *audible*. (audience, heard, seen)

● This author wrote *Rebecca*, about Manderley, Maxim de Winter and the memory of a dead first wife.

■ Narcissus fell in love with a reflection of ? .

▲ A brief form of fiction

⬡ Identify all of the conjunctions in this sentence: Her ring and necklace were lost because I forgot her purse.

● *The Curse of the Blue Figurine* is a very suspenseful gothic story written by this author.

■ What did Pandora leave in her box, trapped forever?

▲ Any writing that uses rhythm and rhyme

⬡ Identify the appositive. My dog, Sandy, is the biggest in the neighborhood.

● Meg, Beth and Amy are three of the March girls in this sentimental romance story. This girl introduces her sisters and other characters.

■ Into what was Narcissus changed while looking into the pool at his reflection.

▲ A story performed on stage

⬡ Pick out the subject of this sentence: Debra found dieting to be rewarding.

● This author wrote *The Murder at the Vicarage*, the first of the Miss Marple mysteries.

■ Which goddess enjoyed gossiping so much she attracted Zeus' attention and entered into a plot against his wife?

▲ Stories that entertain but also explain natural phenomena

⬡ Pick the right spelling of the word meaning "person who has controlling authority." (principal, principle, principel)

● This is the name of Edward Rochester's estate and the setting for *Jane Eyre*.

■ Who extracted a promise from Apollo to ride the golden chariot across the sky and make the sun rise and set?

▲ A printing process that has an important part in the fine arts and in commercial printing

⬡ Pick the correct spelling of this word: curius, curious, cureous.

● A small New England village in the 1800's is the background for this popular book about the March family.

■ With whom did Echo fall in love?

▲ Writing based on fact and true situations

⬡ Identify the interjection in this sentence: Wow! That was a scary movie.

● This story is set in nineteenth century rural England and tells about the lives and loves of the Bennet family.

■ Pyroeis, Eous, Aethon and Phlegon were the names of the four ? that carried Apollo across the sky.

▲ Reason for a character's action

⬡ Identify the predicate in this sentence: I started a checking account today.

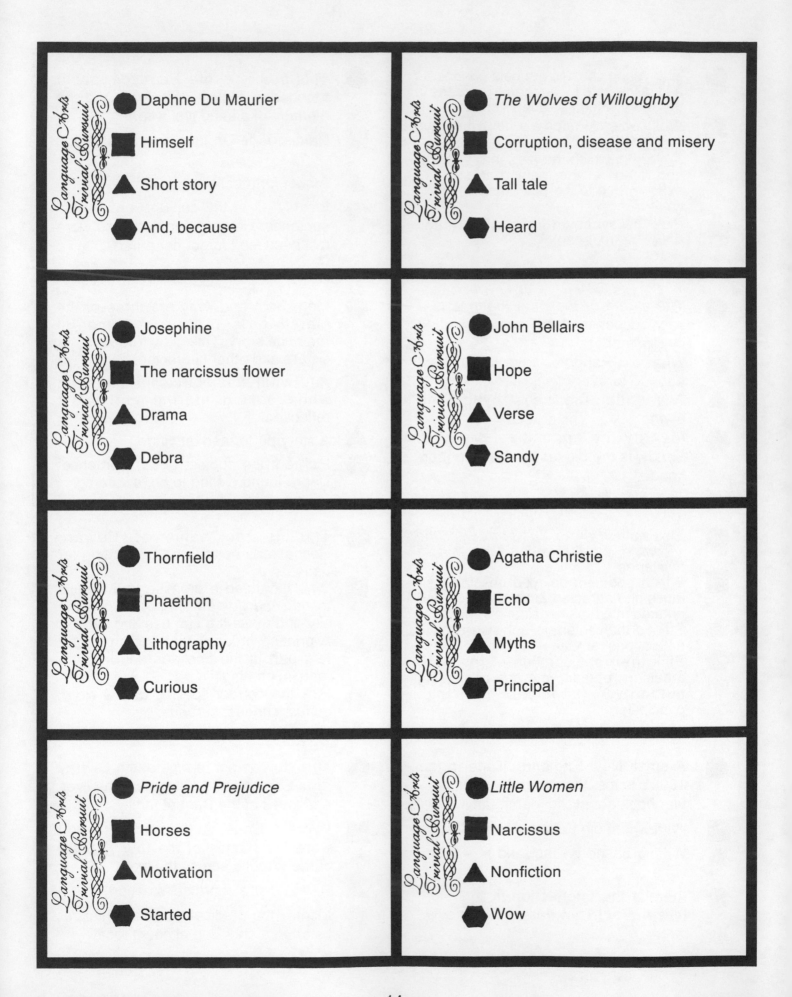

Language Arts Trivial Pursuit

- ● Daphne Du Maurier
- ■ Himself
- ▲ Short story
- ⬡ And, because

Language Arts Trivial Pursuit

- ● *The Wolves of Willoughby*
- ■ Corruption, disease and misery
- ▲ Tall tale
- ⬡ Heard

Language Arts Trivial Pursuit

- ● Josephine
- ■ The narcissus flower
- ▲ Drama
- ⬡ Debra

Language Arts Trivial Pursuit

- ● John Bellairs
- ■ Hope
- ▲ Verse
- ⬡ Sandy

Language Arts Trivial Pursuit

- ● Thornfield
- ■ Phaethon
- ▲ Lithography
- ⬡ Curious

Language Arts Trivial Pursuit

- ● Agatha Christie
- ■ Echo
- ▲ Myths
- ⬡ Principal

Language Arts Trivial Pursuit

- ● *Pride and Prejudice*
- ■ Horses
- ▲ Motivation
- ⬡ Started

Language Arts Trivial Pursuit

- ● *Little Women*
- ■ Narcissus
- ▲ Nonfiction
- ⬡ Wow

● This author wrote *Poseidon Adventure*, which was made into a movie. It is about fifteen people who survive a shipwreck.

■ Who was mother to Phaethon?

▲ The way in which the poet manipulates rhythm, metaphor pattern, to make the poem the utterance that is required

⬡ Give the synonym for *acute*. (collect, sharp, large)

● Jane Eyre becomes the governess of this man's estate.

■ When Daedalus and _?_ were imprisoned in the labyrinth, Daedalus fashioned wings made of wax and feathers and they flew out.

▲ A spell uttered to invite a blessing, to avoid an evil or to call down a malediction

⬡ Put one of these words in the sentence. (their, there, they're) _?_ are 132 rooms in the White House.

● Orphaned and abused, this character spends her early years at the Lowood School.

■ Who is a favorite of Athena to whom she taught mechanical principles?

▲ The letters of the earliest Teutonic alphabet

⬡ Identify the predicate in this sentence: Hundreds of people cleaned up the oil spill.

● This author wrote *Exodus*, which is a novel about the Jews after World War II.

■ _?_, Daedalus' son, flew too close to the sun, melting his wings, and fell into the sea.

▲ This is the American equivalent of the Japanese haiku or tanka.

⬡ Which is the correct analogy for *soar: glide*? (watch:observe, right:wrong, rough:smooth)

● *Pride and Prejudice* focuses on Elizabeth Bennet and this suitor.

■ Who was the son of Zeus and Europa and king of Crete?

▲ Occurs when double or multiple meanings attach to words or to situations

⬡ Put one of these words in the blank (set, sit). Will you _?_ on the sidelines during the entire game?

● H.G. Wells wrote this story about a machine that is able to travel through time.

■ Which son of Zeus was the strongest man in the universe?

▲ A story that teaches a moral

⬡ Use one of these words in the sentence: (lying, laying). They were _?_ in the sun to get a tan.

● This author wrote *Kidnapping Mr. Tubbs*, about a man one hundred years old who is befriended by a young boy and girl.

■ Who was the monster who was half man and half bull, imprisoned in the labyrinth built by Daedalus?

▲ Emphasis on a syllable

⬡ Pick the antonym for *essential*. (different, truthful, unnecessary)

● Heathcliff is the orphan who is taken in by this family in *Wuthering Heights*.

■ Who was the mother of Heracles?

▲ A story about a person's own life

⬡ Use one of these words in the sentence: (sat, set). She _?_ in the rain waiting for a bus.

Language Arts Trivial Pursuit

- ● Edward Rochester
- ■ Icarus
- ▲ Charm
- ⬡ There

Language Arts Trivial Pursuit

- ● Paul Gallico
- ■ Clymene
- ▲ Strategy
- ⬡ Sharp

Language Arts Trivial Pursuit

- ● Leon Uris
- ■ Icarus
- ▲ Cinquain
- ⬡ Watch:observe

Language Arts Trivial Pursuit

- ● Jane Eyre
- ■ Daedalus
- ▲ Runes
- ⬡ Cleaned

Language Arts Trivial Pursuit

- ● *The Time Machine*
- ■ Heracles
- ▲ Fable
- ⬡ Lying

Language Arts Trivial Pursuit

- ● Darcy
- ■ Minos
- ▲ Ambiguity
- ⬡ Sit

Language Arts Trivial Pursuit

- ● Earnshaw family
- ■ Alcmene
- ▲ Autobiography
- ⬡ Sat

Language Arts Trivial Pursuit

- ● Don Schellie
- ■ Minotaur
- ▲ Accent
- ⬡ Unnecessary

GA1384

- ● Clifford Simah wrote this novel that takes place in a world that is still living in the Middle Ages.
- ■ Who was the first wife of Heracles?
- ▲ One of the major divisions of a play
- ⬡ Choose the correct spelling of this word: succede, succeed, suceed.

- ● This author wrote *Dreamsnake*, with the unusual plot about a snake whose venom helps people who are terminally ill.
- ■ Who was the female monster whose hair was entwined with vipers?
- ▲ The part of the play in which the audience is given the background information which it needs to know
- ⬡ Choose the correct spelling of this word: absence, abcense, absance.

- ● This author wrote *The Food of the Gods*, about a world where people never stop growing.
- ■ When Heracles was a babe, what did Kera send into the nursery to kill him and his stepbrother?
- △ An extended narrative that carries a second meaning along with the surface story
- ⬡ Choose one of these words for the sentence: (worse, worst). My cold is _?_ than yours.

- ● This is a mystery novel about a rare yellow diamond with a curse and three Indian guardians sworn to protect it.
- ■ Who was Heracles' second wife and his eventual destruction?
- ▲ A poem in which letters of successive lines form a word or pattern
- ⬡ Pick the correct spelling of the following word: silhouete, silhouette, silouette.

- ● This exciting historical book is about the Indian wars of the 1750's and contains further adventures of Natty Bumpo.
- ■ Eurystheus assigned twelve impossible tasks to _?_ to atone for his harsh and insane acts.
- △ A story of a person's life written by someone else
- ⬡ What is the plural of *salmon*?

- ● This author wrote *The Beginning Place*, about two people in the magical town of Tembreabrezi. They try to save it from certain doom.
- ■ The deadly potion given to Deianeira by the centaur killed _?_.
- ▲ A brief abstract or summary of the plot prefixed to a literary work or to a section of it
- ⬡ Choose *among* or *between* for the blank. Divide the candy _?_ the three of you.

- ● In *Wuthering Heights,* Heathcliff's love for this woman wreaks havoc in the lives of others.
- ■ Whom did Heracles encounter during his eleventh task in order to get at the golden apples of the Hesperides?
- ▲ A literary and artistic movement of the nineteenth century emerging in France
- ⬡ Choose *more* or *most* in the sentence. This tape is _?_ than that one.

- ● This adventure book is about Natty Bumpo and his journey into manhood.
- ■ After Heracles died, Zeus formed him into a _?_.
- ▲ A reference, usually brief, to a presumably familiar person or thing
- ⬡ Pick the synonym for *congested*. (deserted, cleared, clogged)

GA1384

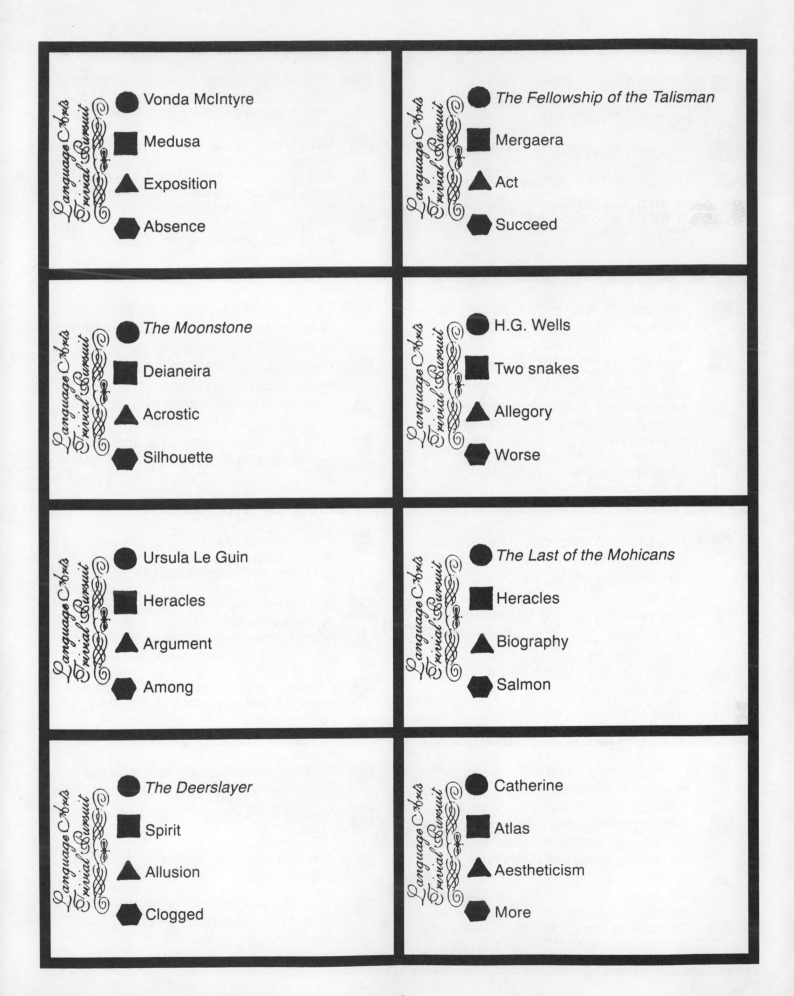

Language Arts Trivial Pursuit

- ● Vonda McIntyre
- ■ Medusa
- ▲ Exposition
- ⬡ Absence

Language Arts Trivial Pursuit

- ● *The Fellowship of the Talisman*
- ■ Mergaera
- ▲ Act
- ⬡ Succeed

Language Arts Trivial Pursuit

- ● *The Moonstone*
- ■ Deianeira
- ▲ Acrostic
- ⬡ Silhouette

Language Arts Trivial Pursuit

- ● H.G. Wells
- ■ Two snakes
- ▲ Allegory
- ⬡ Worse

Language Arts Trivial Pursuit

- ● Ursula Le Guin
- ■ Heracles
- ▲ Argument
- ⬡ Among

Language Arts Trivial Pursuit

- ● *The Last of the Mohicans*
- ■ Heracles
- ▲ Biography
- ⬡ Salmon

Language Arts Trivial Pursuit

- ● *The Deerslayer*
- ■ Spirit
- ▲ Allusion
- ⬡ Clogged

Language Arts Trivial Pursuit

- ● Catherine
- ■ Atlas
- ▲ Aestheticism
- ⬡ More

● This author wrote *Thunderworld*, about four earthlings who are on a planet with strange beings called the Frogroos.

■ Deianeira did this after she killed Heracles in a rage of jealousy.

▲ A word or phrase which is no longer used in actual speech

⬡ Choose *set* or *sit* in the sentence. _?_ the fork on the table.

● This author wrote the book *Escape to Witch Mountain*, about Lea and Tony who came to realize their special gifts are being sought after.

■ He ended the Trojan War and was responsible for the annihilation of Troy.

▲ A yearly record of historical events

⬡ Tell whether these words are antonyms or synonyms. (thoughtful, pensive)

● Natty Bumpo's Indian friend in *The Deerslayer*

■ When Zeus made Heracles into a heavenly spirit after his death, Heracles' mortal past was sent to _?_.

▲ A word or name resulting from the transposition of letters

⬡ Use *leave* or *let* in the sentence. _?_ the back door unlocked when you go.

● This book contains two years of travel records when the author served as a sailor aboard the *Pilgrim*.

■ It was the only vulnerable part on the body of Achilles.

▲ In rhetoric, the repetition of an identical word or group of words in successive verses or clauses

⬡ Use *don't* or *doesn't* in the sentence. A river _?_ always stay within its banks.

● *The Deerslayer* travels through the frontier of this state during the 1740's.

■ Both Poseidon and Zeus wanted to marry her but were frightened by the prophecy that her son would be greater than his father.

▲ A type of hero lacking the usual heroic qualities (such as courage or idealism), frequently a pathetic, comic or antisocial figure

⬡ Pick the antonym for *brevity*. (wordiness, shortness, wittiness)

● This author wrote *The White Dragon*, about a dragon and his rider who have to save their land.

■ She was the goddess of discord.

▲ In literature, a character consisting of certain selected features exaggerated for comic effect

⬡ Spell the plural of *blush*.

● In this book by Steven Crane, Henry Fleming says good-bye to his mother, leaves the farm and goes to fight in the Civil War.

■ Against her will, Thetis was given in marriage to this mortal man.

▲ A word that means the opposite of another

⬡ Use *who* or *whom* in the blank. From _?_ did you borrow the car?

● This is the story in which the main characters are shipwrecked on what appears to be an uninhabited island off the coast of South America.

■ She was the beautiful woman taken as a prize by Achilles.

▲ The close repetition of similar vowel sounds, usually in stressed syllables

⬡ Choose the antonym for *heretic*. (righteous, believer, childish)

19

● Alexander Key

■ Achilles

▲ Annal

⬡ Synonyms

● Zach Hughes

■ Hanged herself

▲ Archaism

⬡ Set

● *Two Years Before the Mast*

■ His heel

▲ Anaphora

⬡ Doesn't

● Chingachgook

■ Hades

▲ Anagram

⬡ Leave

● Anne McCaffery

■ Eris

▲ Caricature

⬡ Blushes

● New York

■ Thetis

▲ Antihero

⬡ Wordiness

● *Robinson Crusoe*

■ Briseis

▲ Assonance

⬡ Believer

● *The Red Badge of Courage*

■ King Peleus

▲ Antonym

⬡ Whom

GA1384

● This author wrote *Around the World in Eighty Days*, about a classic balloon adventure.

■ He was the bravest Trojan warrior and the son of Priam.

▲ Discordant or harsh sounds which are frequently introduced for poetic effect

⬡ Choose the correct pronoun. Has anyone asked to see Marie or (I, me)?

● Who does Robinson Crusoe meet after many years of solitude?

■ These two Greek sources contain most of the basic characters and themes of Greek mythology.

▲ A cul-de-sac, an alley with no outlet

⬡ Add the suffix *ous* to *outrage*.

● *Two Years Before the Mast* depicts the harsh life and injustice faced by the American sailor during which century?

■ He was Achilles' closest friend.

▲ The mood which is established by the totality of a literary work

⬡ Pick the correct word for the sentence. She felt (bad, badly) about rejecting my invitation.

● These authors wrote *When Worlds Collide*, about a group of scientists who have to escape a doomed planet.

■ This group was the most powerful group of Greek divinities

▲ A person whose abilities are concealed until he/she can reveal them to the best advantage

⬡ Correct this misspelled word: *leisurly*.

● This historical romance is set in fifteenth-century France, with Quasimodo the bell ringer as the main character.

■ After the killing of his closest friend, Patroclus, Achilles returned to the _?_ from which he had quit.

▲ A work designed to ridicule attitudes, style or subject matter by handling either an elevated subject in a trivial manner or a low subject with mock dignity

⬡ Pick the synonym for *braggart*. (coward, boaster, daring)

● This author wrote *Lilies of the Field*, about a black war veteran who saves a group of German nuns.

■ The Trojan War was fought between the people of Troy and the people of _?_.

▲ Verse in which the stanzas are linked by rhyme or various patterns of repetition

⬡ What is the purpose of a narrative paragraph? (to tell a story, to explain, to describe)

● This author wrote *Ethan Allan*, about a white family who dares to adopt a black child.

■ This contains the Greek interpretation of creation.

▲ A collection of descriptions of animals

⬡ Spell the plural of *sheaf*.

● This author wrote *The Chocolate War*, about a young boy who dares to challenge the system.

■ The Trojan War began after this woman fled to Troy with Paris, son of the Trojan king.

▲ The quality of internal coherence in the parts of a literary work

⬡ Is the italicized word a noun, a verb, an interjection or a conjunction? *Help*! I'm lost in a maze and can't find my way out!

GA1384

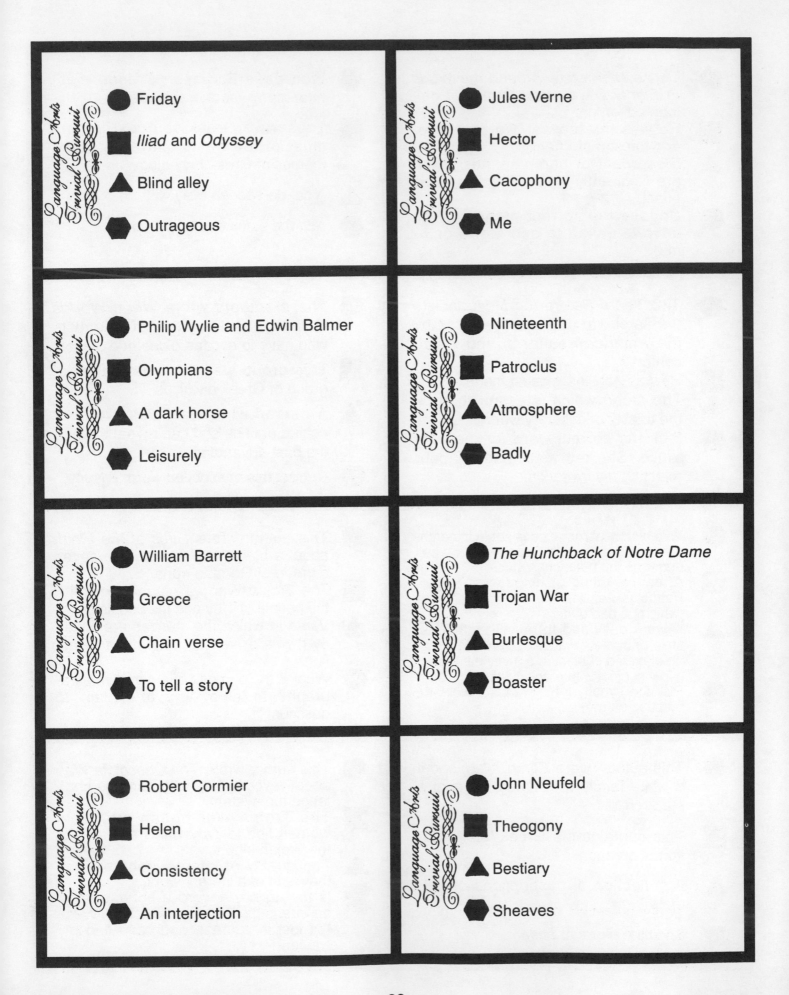

Language Arts Trivial Pursuit

- ● Friday
- ■ *Iliad* and *Odyssey*
- ▲ Blind alley
- ⬡ Outrageous

Language Arts Trivial Pursuit

- ● Jules Verne
- ■ Hector
- ▲ Cacophony
- ⬡ Me

Language Arts Trivial Pursuit

- ● Philip Wylie and Edwin Balmer
- ■ Olympians
- ▲ A dark horse
- ⬡ Leisurely

Language Arts Trivial Pursuit

- ● Nineteenth
- ■ Patroclus
- ▲ Atmosphere
- ⬡ Badly

Language Arts Trivial Pursuit

- ● William Barrett
- ■ Greece
- ▲ Chain verse
- ⬡ To tell a story

Language Arts Trivial Pursuit

- ● *The Hunchback of Notre Dame*
- ■ Trojan War
- ▲ Burlesque
- ⬡ Boaster

Language Arts Trivial Pursuit

- ● Robert Cormier
- ■ Helen
- ▲ Consistency
- ⬡ An interjection

Language Arts Trivial Pursuit

- ● John Neufeld
- ■ Theogony
- ▲ Bestiary
- ⬡ Sheaves

GA1384

● Esmeralda, a beautiful gypsy, and this evil archdeacon of Notre Dame are two main characters in *The Hunchback of Notre Dame*.

■ This goddess was one of the few divinities that sided with Troy.

▲ An underhanded plot, a piece of crafty maneuvering or a liaison

⬢ Pick the correct synonym for *spherical*. (rotating, difference, globular)

● These authors wrote *Grover*, which describes Grover adjusting to his mother's death.

■ The earliest information we have about Egyptian mythology comes from this type of writing on the walls of tombs.

▲ A person always poring over books

⬢ Add the suffix *er* to *shop*.

● The main characters of this book are the governess Bly and her charges Miles and Flora.

■ These three gods became associated with the twelve Olympians.

▲ High or noble birth or descent

⬢ Choose the correct antonym for *solicitous*. (flexible, neglectful, occupied)

● This black man, accused of rape, creates a stir in *To Kill a Mockingbird*.

■ These are gods who take on the shape of man.

▲ The Monday before Lent spent in dissipation

⬢ The noun that a pronoun refers to or replaces is called its __?__.

● This author wrote *Tiger Eyes*, about Darsey Wiler who goes through a painful period of adjusting to her father's death.

■ The partly mortal and partly divine beings were given this name.

▲ A record of events in historical order

⬢ Choose the correct analogy for *bark:tree*. (wax:furniture, jacket:coat, crash:train)

● This author wrote *Sunshine*, about a woman who had to face death at the early age of twenty.

■ These are gods who resemble animals.

▲ The method of adjusting for omitted unstressed syllables in a line of metrical verse

⬢ Choose the correct antonym for *flippant*. (changeable, serious, deceitful)

● Atticus Finch, the main character in this book, defends a black man who is accused of rape.

■ This temple is one of the Seven Wonders of the World.

▲ The implications or suggestions that are evoked by a word

⬢ Choose the correct synonym for *insatiable*. (satisfied, greedy, eccentric)

● In this book, the wolf-like Buck is stolen and made to face a life of an Alaskan sled huskie in the 1890's.

■ This is the most sacred place in Japanese mythology.

▲ A timeworn expression which has lost its vitality and, to some extent, its original meaning

⬢ Identify the antecedent for *her* in this sentence: Jenny carried her lunch box to school.

GA1384

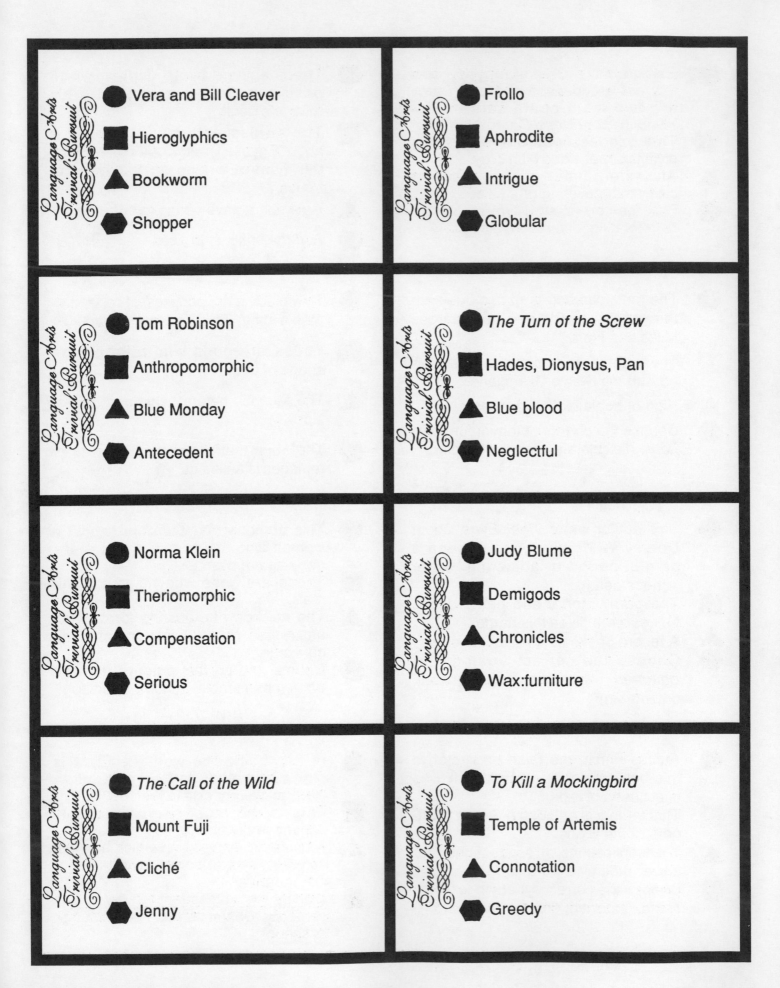

Language Arts Trivial Pursuit

- ● Vera and Bill Cleaver
- ■ Hieroglyphics
- ▲ Bookworm
- ⬡ Shopper

Language Arts Trivial Pursuit

- ● Frollo
- ■ Aphrodite
- ▲ Intrigue
- ⬡ Globular

Language Arts Trivial Pursuit

- ● Tom Robinson
- ■ Anthropomorphic
- ▲ Blue Monday
- ⬡ Antecedent

Language Arts Trivial Pursuit

- ● *The Turn of the Screw*
- ■ Hades, Dionysus, Pan
- ▲ Blue blood
- ⬡ Neglectful

Language Arts Trivial Pursuit

- ● Norma Klein
- ■ Theriomorphic
- ▲ Compensation
- ⬡ Serious

Language Arts Trivial Pursuit

- ● Judy Blume
- ■ Demigods
- ▲ Chronicles
- ⬡ Wax:furniture

Language Arts Trivial Pursuit

- ● *The Call of the Wild*
- ■ Mount Fuji
- ▲ Cliché
- ⬡ Jenny

Language Arts Trivial Pursuit

- ● *To Kill a Mockingbird*
- ■ Temple of Artemis
- ▲ Connotation
- ⬡ Greedy

● This author wrote *Red Sky at Morning*, about a boy growing up in New Mexico.

■ He killed Achilles by shooting an arrow and mortally wounding him in the heel.

▲ Something that is hard to understand

⬢ Pick the correct analogy for *snow: shovel*. (wash:dirt, grass:lawn mower, cook:food)

● This author wrote *Dolphin Island* about a group of scientists who work with dolphins.

■ Aphrodite offered this queen as a prize to Paris for selecting her as the fairest of women.

▲ Rhymeless verse in continued decasyllables with iambic or trochaic rhythm

⬢ Identify the pronouns in this sentence: They carried their raincoats with them.

● This man meets and befriends Buck in *The Call of the Wild*.

■ This expression describes a person's particular weakness or vulnerable spot.

▲ A paragraph printed on the dust wrapper or in the preliminary pages of a book purporting to tell what the book is about

⬢ Add the suffix *able* to *rely*.

● This author wrote *The Deep*, about a struggle between Red men and Black men.

■ These brothers banded together to battle for the return of Helen from Troy.

▲ An evil character who acts in opposition to the hero

⬢ Choose the synonym for *intrinsic*. (essential, opposite, troubled)

● This author wrote *Planet of the Apes*, about a trip into the future where the apes are superior beings.

■ The only one not invited to the regal marriage ceremony of Thetis and Peleus

▲ Any literary work, less exalted and less serious than a tragedy, usually with a happy ending

⬢ Choose the antonym for *naive*. (sophisticated, cruel, direct)

● This is George Orwell's satire of a totalitarian society.

■ She was the face that launched a thousand ships.

▲ The speeches of characters in a narrative or a play

⬢ Pick the correct analogy for *rules: teacher*. (wax:furniture, laws:police, books:covers)

● In this book, Frank Bonham tells how Rufus Henry has to make the choice of joining a gang for protection or being sent back to the home for delinquents.

■ At the wedding of Thetis and Peleus, Eris set this down in the midst of Athena, Hera and Aphrodite with the message "to the fairest."

▲ A word of uncertain origin, originally signifying a small dagger

⬢ Spell the plural of *moose*.

● This author wrote *Ivanhoe*, a classic story with the setting during the time of the Crusades.

■ He was the wisest Greek strategist of the Trojan War who decided to use the wooden horse.

▲ A generally accepted literary device or form

⬢ Pick the antonym for *impartial*. (whole, unfair, stubborn)

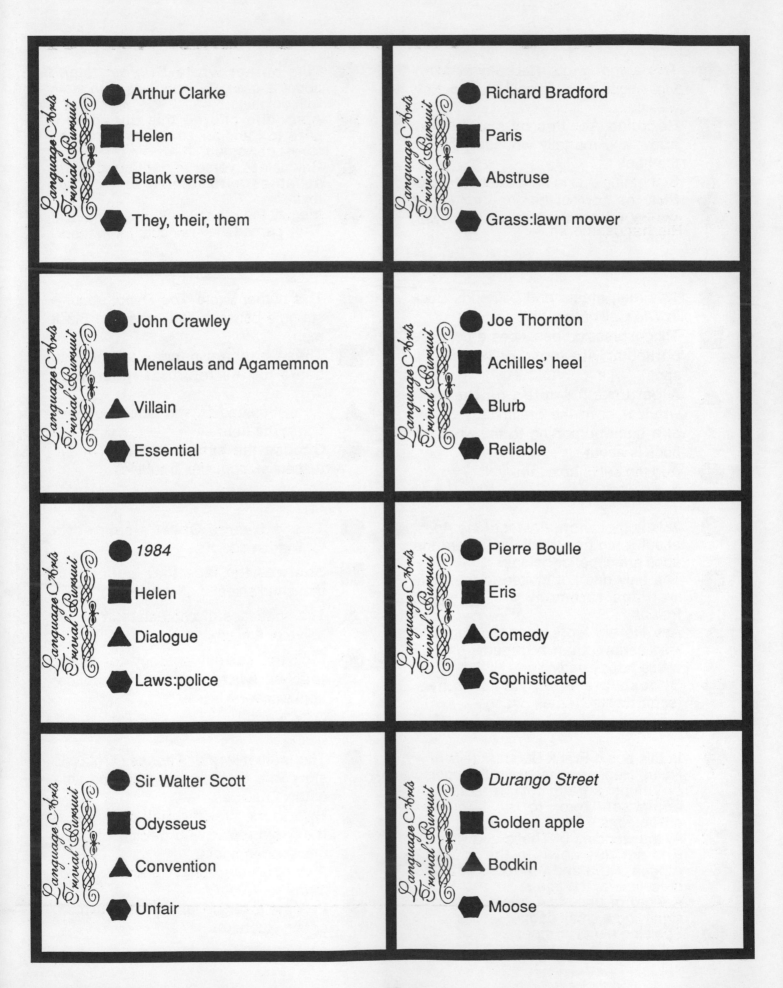

Language Arts Trivial Pursuit

● Arthur Clarke

■ Helen

▲ Blank verse

⬡ They, their, them

Language Arts Trivial Pursuit

● Richard Bradford

■ Paris

▲ Abstruse

⬡ Grass:lawn mower

Language Arts Trivial Pursuit

● John Crawley

■ Menelaus and Agamemnon

▲ Villain

⬡ Essential

Language Arts Trivial Pursuit

● Joe Thornton

■ Achilles' heel

▲ Blurb

⬡ Reliable

Language Arts Trivial Pursuit

● *1984*

■ Helen

▲ Dialogue

⬡ Laws:police

Language Arts Trivial Pursuit

● Pierre Boulle

■ Eris

▲ Comedy

⬡ Sophisticated

Language Arts Trivial Pursuit

● Sir Walter Scott

■ Odysseus

▲ Convention

⬡ Unfair

Language Arts Trivial Pursuit

● *Durango Street*

■ Golden apple

▲ Bodkin

⬡ Moose

GA1384

- In this book, the main character discovers the secret of creating life and makes a creature out of materials collected from butchers and dissection labs.
- He was the one cautious voice after the wooden horse was wheeled in that said, "Beware of Greeks bearing gifts."
- The Greek from which this word comes means "evil speaking."
- Identify the adjectives in this sentence: His handsome smile lit up his whole face.

- This novel by Joseph Conrad describes life in the Dutch East Indies in the nineteenth century.
- From where in Greek mythology did we get the word *chronology*?
- To put in between other ideas and words
- Identify the antecedent for the italicized word. John caught the Frisbee and threw *it* to me.

- This author wrote *The White Stag* about the migration of Hungarians to new frontiers.
- Agamemnon, a commander during the Trojan War, was killed after the war by this woman.
- Breaking up of anything complex into its various simple elements
- Choose the synonym for *flabbergasted*. (expanded, complimented, astonished)

- This author wrote *Rags to Riches*, about Julie Mahoney and the problems with great wealth and possessions.
- From where in Greek mythology did we get the word *cloth*?
- A reasonable conclusion drawn by the reader or viewer from hints or implications provided by the author
- Identify the antecedent of the italicized pronoun. Sean took three suitcases with *him* to Florida.

- This is a nineteenth century tale of a vampire who lives off the blood of his victims.
- In Greek mythology, the word *ambrosia* refers to food and drink of _?_.
- Two successive lines of verse, usually rhymed and of the same meter
- Identify the antecedent for the italicized pronoun. The ocean has a green tint to *it*.

- This work of Charles Dickens was a favorite of his. It is a story of an abandoned waif who learns to deal with life's challenges.
- From where in Greek mythology did we get the word *erratic*?
- The evaluation of literary works
- Pick the correct word to finish this sentence: Are (their, they're) shoes dry yet?

- This author wrote *Uncle Tom's Cabin*, a story about the horrors of slavery.
- From where in Roman mythology do we get the word *cereal*?
- Details of a time, place, character and social setting which create the "world" in which a story moves
- Pick *who* or *whom* to begin this sentence: _?_ is on the phone?

- This author wrote *The Best Christmas Pageant Ever*, about a rowdy group of kids who decide they want to be in a Christmas pageant.
- From where in Greek mythology did we get the word *tantalize*?
- Any period in art or literature which is in decline as compared with a former age of excellence
- Choose the correct word to complete this sentence: Of the three trails, which one is the (more, most) scenic?

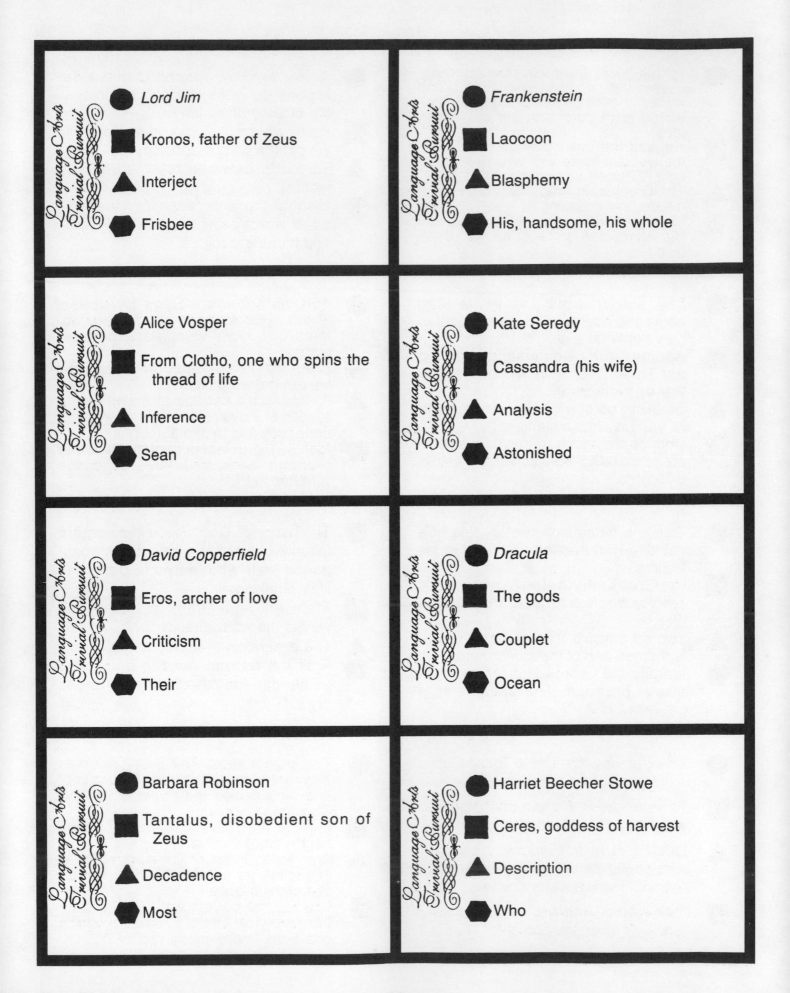

Language Arts Trivial Pursuit

- ● *Lord Jim*
- ■ Kronos, father of Zeus
- ▲ Interject
- ⬡ Frisbee

Language Arts Trivial Pursuit

- ● *Frankenstein*
- ■ Laocoon
- ▲ Blasphemy
- ⬡ His, handsome, his whole

Language Arts Trivial Pursuit

- ● Alice Vosper
- ■ From Clotho, one who spins the thread of life
- ▲ Inference
- ⬡ Sean

Language Arts Trivial Pursuit

- ● Kate Seredy
- ■ Cassandra (his wife)
- ▲ Analysis
- ⬡ Astonished

Language Arts Trivial Pursuit

- ● *David Copperfield*
- ■ Eros, archer of love
- ▲ Criticism
- ⬡ Their

Language Arts Trivial Pursuit

- ● *Dracula*
- ■ The gods
- ▲ Couplet
- ⬡ Ocean

Language Arts Trivial Pursuit

- ● Barbara Robinson
- ■ Tantalus, disobedient son of Zeus
- ▲ Decadence
- ⬡ Most

Language Arts Trivial Pursuit

- ● Harriet Beecher Stowe
- ■ Ceres, goddess of harvest
- ▲ Description
- ⬡ Who

GA1384

● This author was born in 1812 in Landport, Portsea, England. His first-hand knowledge of hunger, deprivation and the horror of debtor's prison was reflected in his writing.

■ From where in Greek mythology did we get the word *hypnosis*?

▲ An author's expressed attitude toward the subject in a literary work

⬡ Complete the analogy: Like is to likely as definite is to ? .

● Who is the main character in *Where the Red Fern Grows*?

■ They became the twin stars, forming the constellation of Gemini.

▲ Sometimes used to indicate the subject of a work

⬡ Give the homonym for *see*.

● This author wrote *Freaky Friday*, about the role change between a thirteen-year-old and her mother.

■ From where in Greek mythology did we get the word *panic*?

▲ A poem comprising seven sonnets, which are interlinked

⬡ Choose the correct word to complete this sentence: (Most, More) households have more than one pet.

● This author was born in 1919 and spent much of his childhood exploring the hills and valleys of the Ozarks, the setting for his first novel.

■ Killing the sea monster, Perseus carried her away, and she became his bride.

▲ As used in France, referred to comic or satirical songs about well-known personalities

⬡ Complete the analogy. Inspiration is to inspire as perspiration is to ? .

● This book is set in the mountain country of the Ozarks. The main character tells of his dream to own and train a fine hunting dog.

■ From where in Greek mythology did we get the word *psychology*?

▲ The choice and arrangement of words in a literary work

⬡ Complete the analogy with the correct answer. Whole is to eight as fraction is to (ten, two-thirds).

● This author wrote *How Green Was My Valley*, about life in a Welsh mining town.

■ She boasted to the sea nymphs that she and her daughter, Andromeda, were far more beautiful.

▲ A publication devoted entirely to a shortened form of books or articles that have already appeared

⬡ Identify the adjective in the following sentence: Lightning may strike the telephone lines!

● This author wrote *Devil in Vienna*, about two girls during World War who found themselves on opposing sides.

■ Each one had only one eye in the middle of his forehead.

▲ The total number of copies of a work printed from a single set of type

⬡ Choose the antonym for *improvise*. (plan, shady, required)

● He was an American writer of science fiction and nonfiction. His most popular work is the *Foundation Series*.

■ He sent a huge, hungry sea monster to Ethiopia to devour King Cepheus' people.

▲ A line and then an *echo* which repeats the final syllables with a change in meaning

⬡ Complete the analogy: Pleased is to displeased as satisfied is to ? .

GA1384

Language Arts Trivial Pursuit

- ● Billy Calmon
- ■ Castor and Pollux
- ▲ Theme
- ⬡ Sea

Language Arts Trivial Pursuit

- ● Charles Dickens
- ■ Hypnos, god of sleep
- ▲ Tone
- ⬡ Definitely

Language Arts Trivial Pursuit

- ● Wilson Rawls
- ■ Andromeda
- ▲ Vaudeville
- ⬡ Perspire

Language Arts Trivial Pursuit

- ● Mary Rodgers
- ■ Pan, god of shepherds and goat herds
- ▲ Crown of sonnets
- ⬡ Most

Language Arts Trivial Pursuit

- ● Richard Llewellyn
- ■ Cassiopeia
- ▲ Digest
- ⬡ Telephone

Language Arts Trivial Pursuit

- ● *Where the Red Fern Grows*
- ■ Psyche, mortal wife of Eros
- ▲ Diction
- ⬡ Two-thirds

Language Arts Trivial Pursuit

- ● Isaac Asimov
- ■ Poseidon
- ▲ Echo verse
- ⬡ Dissatisfied

Language Arts Trivial Pursuit

- ● Katherine Peterson
- ■ Cyclops
- ▲ Edition
- ⬡ Plan

● This author wrote the classic *Gone with the Wind* which was eventually made into a world-famous movie.

■ He could walk on water, a gift given to him by his father, Poseidon.

▲ A proposition to be maintained

⬡ Spell a homonym for *deer*.

● This author wrote *The Castaway*, a familiar plot but true story of a sailor shipwrecked on an island in the South Pacific.

■ He was the son of King Adson of Iolcus and was brought up by Chiron the Centaur to escape death by King Pelias.

▲ A brief essay, usually in the form of a pamphlet on a religious or political subject

⬡ Pick out the direct object of this sentence: The pitcher threw David a fastball.

● *Pride and Prejudice* was this woman's first novel.

■ To win her hand in marriage, Orion had to rid the island of Chios of lions, bears and wolves.

▲ A member of the class of lyric poets whose activities were centered in southern France in the twelfth and thirteenth centuries

⬡ Complete the analogy: Legally is to legality as really is to __?__.

● Geoffrey Chaucer wrote this collection of separate stories, many of which were very humorous.

■ King Pelias was warned that he would be killed by a relative wearing one of these.

▲ Language which departs from its literal meaning

⬡ Give the homonym for *poll*.

● This author wrote *Of Nightingales That Weep*, about a samurai's daughter, set in feudal Japan.

■ After Orion gave up his search for Merope, he spent his days hunting with this goddess of the hunt.

▲ Theoretical rather than practical

⬡ Give the homonym for *root*.

● This author wrote *The Good Earth* about a Chinese peasant and his family who struggle to survive.

■ When Jason claimed his title of King, King Pelias asked him to bring this back from the kingdom of Colchis.

▲ Two metrical feet considered as a unit

⬡ Pick the indirect object of this sentence: I gave the cashier the check for our tickets.

● Miguel de Cervantes wrote this popular book about a dreamer and a realist who rode the roads of Spain long ago.

■ Bent on destroying Orion, this jealous god challenged Artemis to hit a mark at sea, which she did. It turned out to be Orion whom she had killed.

▲ A verse of two metrical feet

⬡ Pick the correct preposition for this sentence: A disagreement arose (between, among) the four coaches.

● The Charles Dickens' story about a man who, because of his greedy nature, tries to ruin Christmas.

■ The ship *Argo*, which called for fifty volunteers, was built for Jason to capture the *Golden Fleece*. These men were called __?__.

▲ In verse, three lines which constitute a unit

⬡ Give the homonym for *taught*.

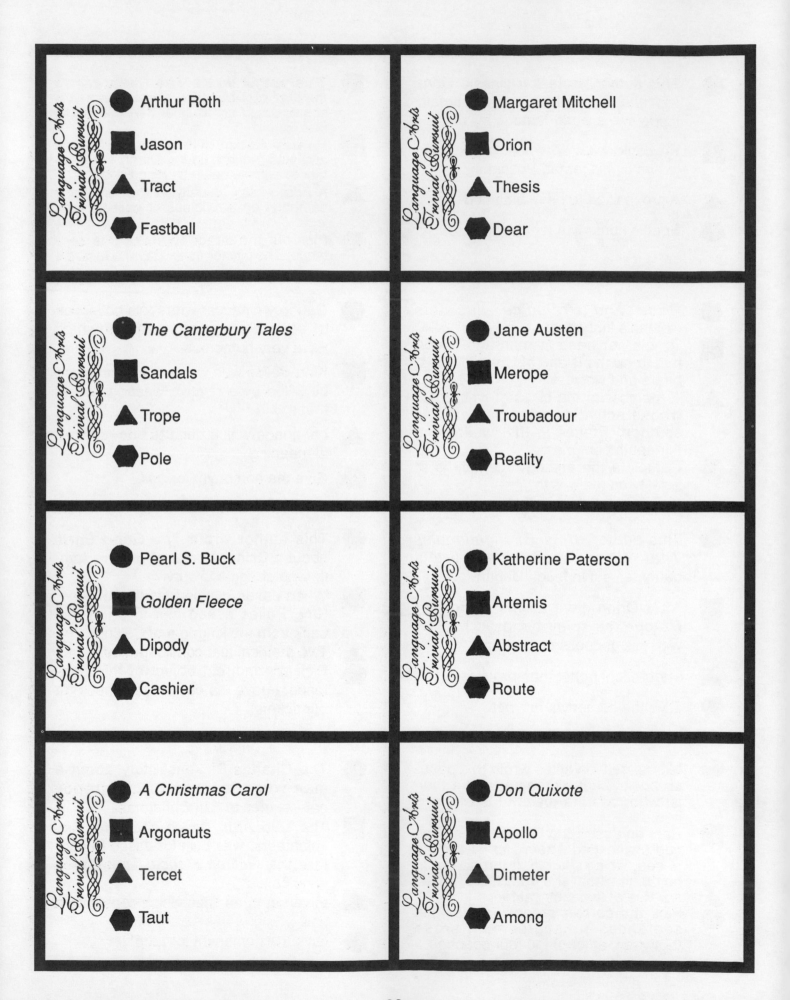

Language Arts Trivial Pursuit

● Arthur Roth
■ Jason
▲ Tract
⬢ Fastball

Language Arts Trivial Pursuit

● Margaret Mitchell
■ Orion
▲ Thesis
⬢ Dear

Language Arts Trivial Pursuit

● *The Canterbury Tales*
■ Sandals
▲ Trope
⬢ Pole

Language Arts Trivial Pursuit

● Jane Austen
■ Merope
▲ Troubadour
⬢ Reality

Language Arts Trivial Pursuit

● Pearl S. Buck
■ *Golden Fleece*
▲ Dipody
⬢ Cashier

Language Arts Trivial Pursuit

● Katherine Paterson
■ Artemis
▲ Abstract
⬢ Route

Language Arts Trivial Pursuit

● *A Christmas Carol*
■ Argonauts
▲ Tercet
⬢ Taut

Language Arts Trivial Pursuit

● *Don Quixote*
■ Apollo
▲ Dimeter
⬢ Among

GA1384

- This author wrote *The Citadel*, about a young doctor who is in conflict with the establishment.
- Because of his inability to predict the future, Zeus punishes this ruler by starving him.
- A brief story, play or essay not as fully developed as the typical examples of these genres
- Pick out the nouns in this sentence: The rain beat steadily against the roof.

- This story, by E.B. White, is a brilliant web woven around a pig, a spider and a rat.
- What was the *Golden Fleece* guarded by?
- Low comedy characterized by physical action, such as the throwing of custard pies
- Pick out the correct word for this sentence: She told how (her, she) and her husband flew to Russia.

- This author came up with the popular imaginary hero Sherlock Holmes.
- Because of his inability to predict the future, these two horrible flying creatures steal Phineus' meal each day.
- A play which evokes laughter by a variety of devices
- Pick out the compound predicate in this sentence: Phil swept and washed the floor.

- This author wrote *The Count of Monte Cristo*, the classic story of revenge.
- She was a witch who was the only one who could help the Argonauts with their dangerous mission.
- Rhyme which is obvious to the eye but not to the ear
- Pick out the correct word for this sentence: Have you finished (your, you're) homework for tomorrow?

- The hero of these tales that take place in India is Mowgli. He is an abandoned white child who was brought up and educated by wolves.
- These two men chase away the Harpies as a favor to Phineus.
- An extended narrative poem, exalted in style and heroic in theme
- Choose the correct analogy for *stair:stare*. (high:huge, one:won, cup:cap)

- When one cannot see, hear or speak, a miracle needs to happen and this book is about just such a miracle.
- He shot an arrow of love into Medea's heart so she could help Jason with his mission.
- A short, usually witty statement, graceful in style and clever in thought
- Pick the correct homonym for this sentence: After rush hour, the traffic will (lessen, lesson) in the downtown area.

- This is the author of *Death of a Salesman*. He creates a tragedy around Willy, who is a man whose ideas about himself and the world are deeply flawed.
- The Argonauts got through the Symplegades, or Clashing Islands, by sending what through first?
- A stationary, silent grouping of actors and actresses in a theatrical production for special effect
- Choose the correct word to use in this sentence: To (who, whom) did you give the application?

- This author wrote *The Good Shepherd*, about World War II.
- What promise did Medea extract from Jason in exchange for her help?
- A group of lines which form a division of a poem
- Identify the misspelled plural noun and spell it correctly. When you fish, stay out of the bushs.

GA1384

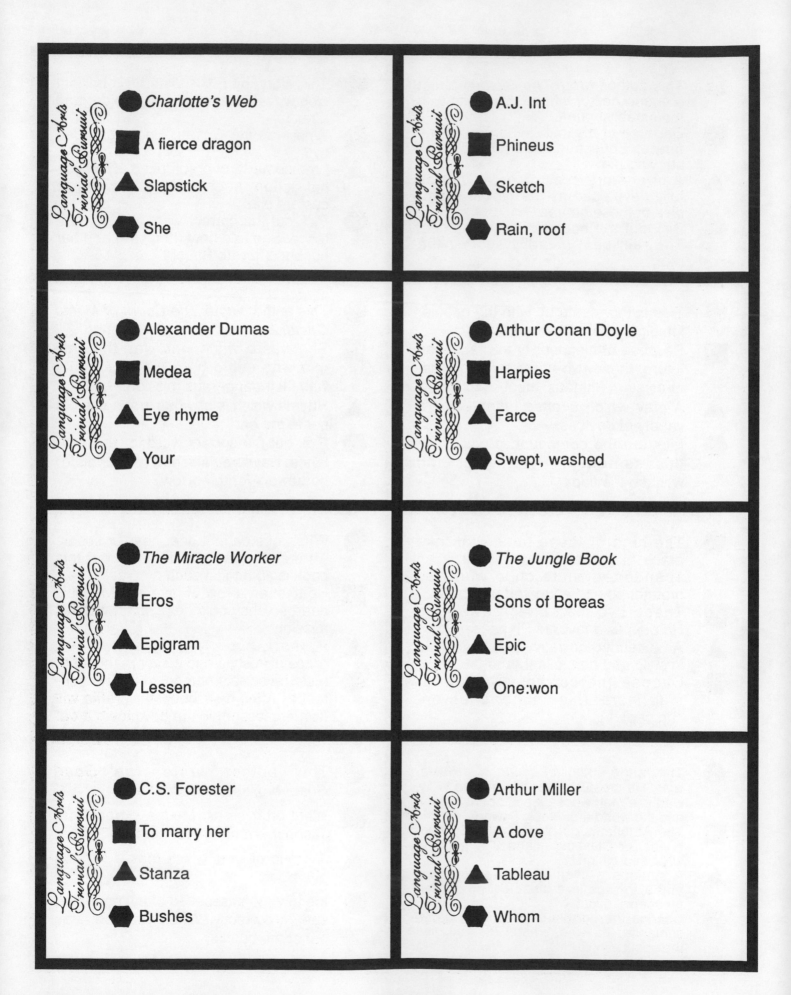

Language Arts Trivial Pursuit

● *Charlotte's Web*

■ A fierce dragon

▲ Slapstick

⬡ She

Language Arts Trivial Pursuit

● A.J. Int

■ Phineus

▲ Sketch

⬡ Rain, roof

Language Arts Trivial Pursuit

● Alexander Dumas

■ Medea

▲ Eye rhyme

⬡ Your

Language Arts Trivial Pursuit

● Arthur Conan Doyle

■ Harpies

▲ Farce

⬡ Swept, washed

Language Arts Trivial Pursuit

● *The Miracle Worker*

■ Eros

▲ Epigram

⬡ Lessen

Language Arts Trivial Pursuit

● *The Jungle Book*

■ Sons of Boreas

▲ Epic

⬡ One:won

Language Arts Trivial Pursuit

● C.S. Forester

■ To marry her

▲ Stanza

⬡ Bushes

Language Arts Trivial Pursuit

● Arthur Miller

■ A dove

▲ Tableau

⬡ Whom

GA1384

■ It is on the moors of Devonshire in southwest England that Sir Arthur Conan Doyle sets this mystery suspense story involving the famous Sherlock Holmes.

■ He was Medea's brother, and he was sent with an army to reclaim the *Golden Fleece*.

▲ An object that signifies something else Pick the correct homonym to complete this: The dog got his (tail, tale) caught in the door.

● This book is about a poor woodcutter who, from a hiding place, observes robbers concealing their spoils.

■ The son of Aethra and Aegeus who grew up not knowing who his father was.

▲ An adjective or other term used to characterize a person or thing

⬡ Identify the plural noun that is misspelled and correct it. The store was full of stereoes.

● This author wrote *The Unicorn in the Garden*, about someone waking up, looking out the window and seeing something that does not exist.

■ She sent Jason's new bride a beautiful robe that she sprinkled with poison.

▲ The final section of a speech

⬡ What is the meaning of the suffix *ment*?

● She wrote *Blubber*, the story of a friend who stands up for an obese classmate.

■ The moment Theseus rolled back the rock and found a pair of sandals and glittering sword, this secret was revealed to him by his mother.

▲ An incident within a longer narrative, sometimes closely connected to the plot, sometimes a digression

⬡ What is the meaning of the suffix *ing*?

● This classical tale by Lewis Carroll had main characters such as the White Rabbit and the Cheshire Cat.

□ When this friendless, homeless old man returned to his ship, the *Argo*, the prow fell on his head and he died.

△ A poem in which a long verse is followed by a shorter one

⬡ Identify the interjection in this sentence: Surprise! We baked the cake after all.

● This Danish writer is the author of over 150 fairy stories and other tales. One of his last stories was *The Cripple*.

■ She arranged for King Aegeus to poison his own son because she was afraid of losing her position of influence with him.

▲ A verse letter

⬡ Choose the correct word. The lemon frosting (affected, effected) the taste of the cake.

● This author wrote the classic *The Sword in the Stone*.

■ Princess Aethra of Troezen was secretly married to this king.

▲ In a literary work, an expectant uncertainty concerning the outcome of the plot

⬡ Pick the correct homonym to complete this sentence: Geologists found gold in a (load, lode) that was very obvious.

● This author wrote the ever-popular *Bedknobs and Broomsticks.*

■ This father, seeing the sword on the table, realized Theseus was his son.

▲ The songs, stories, myths and proverbs of a people handed down by word of mouth

⬡ What is the meaning of the prefix *re*?

GA1384

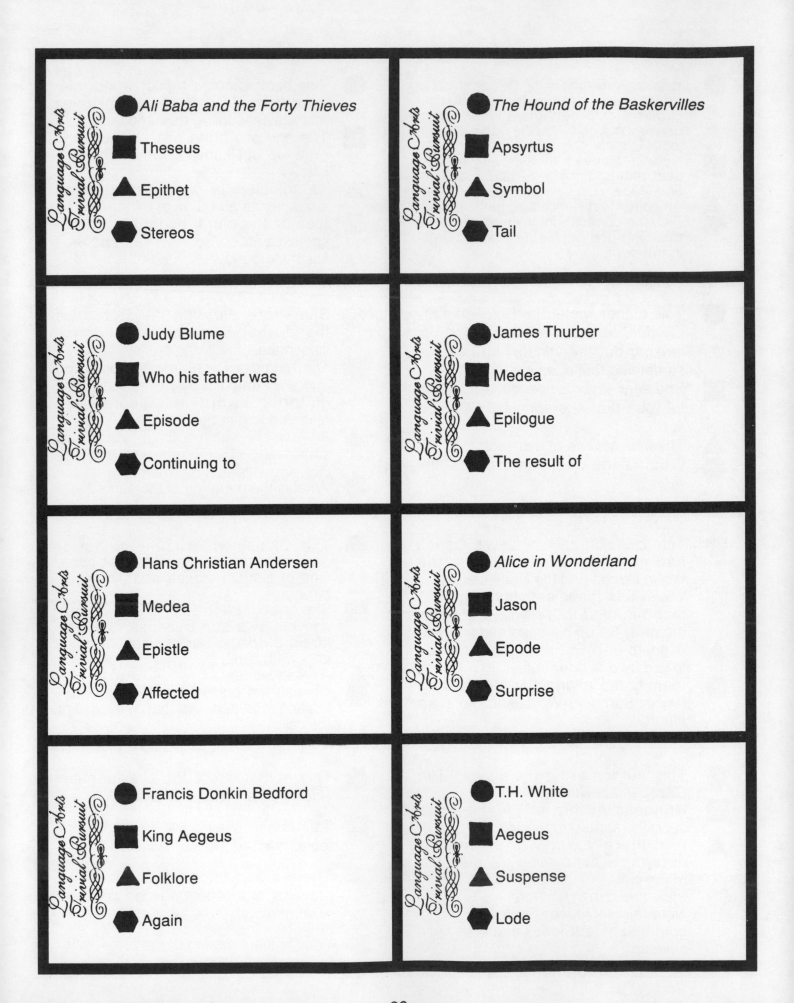

Language Arts Trivial Pursuit

● *Ali Baba and the Forty Thieves*

■ Theseus

▲ Epithet

⬡ Stereos

Language Arts Trivial Pursuit

● *The Hound of the Baskervilles*

■ Apsyrtus

▲ Symbol

⬡ Tail

Language Arts Trivial Pursuit

● Judy Blume

■ Who his father was

▲ Episode

⬡ Continuing to

Language Arts Trivial Pursuit

● James Thurber

■ Medea

▲ Epilogue

⬡ The result of

Language Arts Trivial Pursuit

● Hans Christian Andersen

■ Medea

▲ Epistle

⬡ Affected

Language Arts Trivial Pursuit

● *Alice in Wonderland*

■ Jason

▲ Epode

⬡ Surprise

Language Arts Trivial Pursuit

● Francis Donkin Bedford

■ King Aegeus

▲ Folklore

⬡ Again

Language Arts Trivial Pursuit

● T.H. White

■ Aegeus

▲ Suspense

⬡ Lode

- This book, written by Anna Sewell, was the most celebrated animal story of the nineteenth century.
- This daughter of Demeter loved springtime and flowers and running outdoors with her friends.
- Suggests the secondhand and derivative rather than the original
- Choose the correct word. What (advice, advise) did you give your daughter?

- This author wrote *Pilgrim's Progress*, about Christian and his journey to the Celestial City.
- Pygmalion was a (singer, sculptor, painter, harpist).
- A fixed metrical arrangement, such as the sonnet or the ballad
- What does the suffix *able* mean?

- This author wrote the popular *The Chosen*, about two Jewish boys who become friends despite the differences in their family backgrounds.
- Who is the Roman god of agriculture?
- A poem or stanza of six lines
- Identify an adverb in this sentence: Soon he will play the piano again.

- This author wrote *Pinocchio*, the classic tale of a puppet
- Pygmalion's true love's name was (Hera, Aphrodite, Athena, Galetea).
- In Greek drama, a comic afterpiece concerned with animals or satyrs, creatures half-man and half-goat
- Choose the correct word. It is hard to (accept, except) a compliment graciously.

- This author wrote *The Bridge over the River Kwai,* about prisoners during World War II who were forced to build a bridge.
- Who is the Roman god of fortune?
- Ridicule of any subject
- Choose the correct word. The scene gave the (illusion, allusion) of dance ghosts.

- This author wrote *The Twenty-One Balloons*, a story about the rescue of Professor William Sherman.
- The goddess that gave life to Pygmalion's statue was (Demeter, Hermes, Aphrodite, Artemis).
- A poem or stanza of seven lines
- Choose the synonym for *malevolent*. (remiss, spiteful, frivolous)

- This author wrote *The Last Unicorn*, a fantasy about a unicorn's search for her lost friends.
- Who is the Roman god of spring?
- The most ordinary of the terms meaning "the laughable"
- What does the prefix *de* mean?

- This author wrote *Lost Horizon*, a story of Hugh Conway's journey to where time stands still and people do not age.
- A chimaera has all but which one of the following: the head of a lion, the tail of a serpent, the feet of a horse, the body of a goat?
- Complete or total truth
- Write the correct analogy for *gasoline:motor*. (hate:enemy, food:body, airplane:rocket)

GA1384

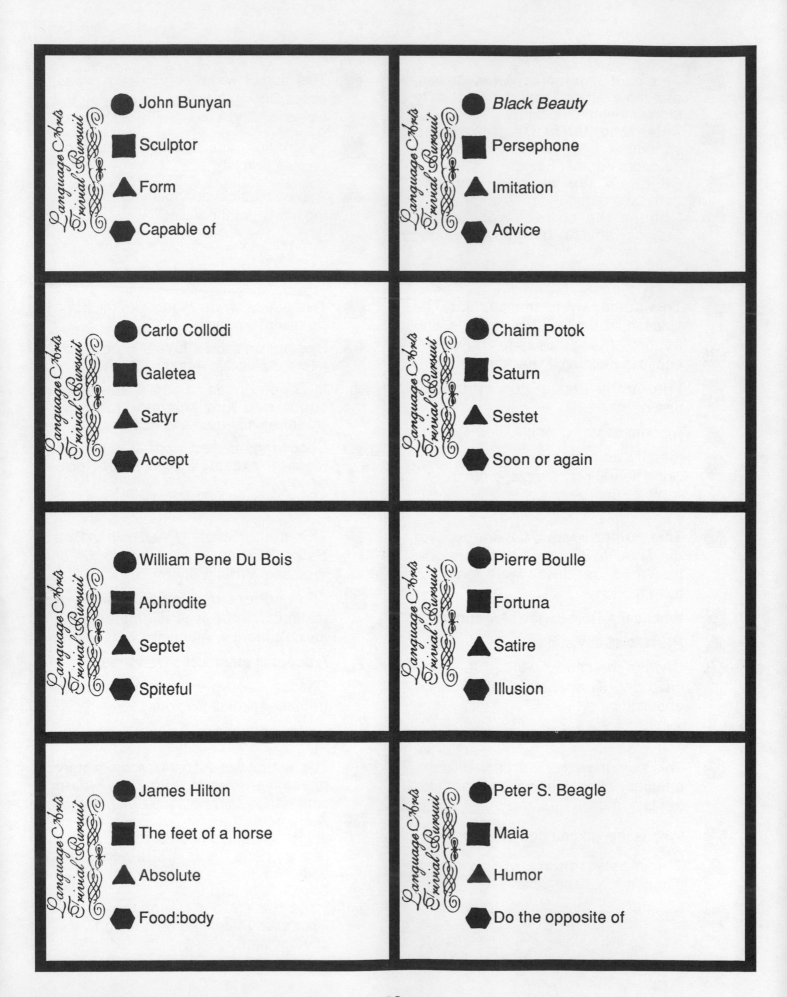

Language Arts Trivial Pursuit

- ● John Bunyan
- ■ Sculptor
- ▲ Form
- ⬡ Capable of

Language Arts Trivial Pursuit

- ● *Black Beauty*
- ■ Persephone
- ▲ Imitation
- ⬡ Advice

Language Arts Trivial Pursuit

- ● Carlo Collodi
- ■ Galetea
- ▲ Satyr
- ⬡ Accept

Language Arts Trivial Pursuit

- ● Chaim Potok
- ■ Saturn
- ▲ Sestet
- ⬡ Soon or again

Language Arts Trivial Pursuit

- ● William Pene Du Bois
- ■ Aphrodite
- ▲ Septet
- ⬡ Spiteful

Language Arts Trivial Pursuit

- ● Pierre Boulle
- ■ Fortuna
- ▲ Satire
- ⬡ Illusion

Language Arts Trivial Pursuit

- ● James Hilton
- ■ The feet of a horse
- ▲ Absolute
- ⬡ Food:body

Language Arts Trivial Pursuit

- ● Peter S. Beagle
- ■ Maia
- ▲ Humor
- ⬡ Do the opposite of

● This author wrote *Animal Farm*, a story involving animals, to explain the history of communism.

■ Bellerophon killed the chimaera by (shooting it with arrows, burning it, throwing if off the cliff, stoning it).

▲ Novels and stories dealing with the achievements of science

⬡ Pick the correct word. The dog (adapted, adopted) to his new environment quickly.

● This book by Sheila Burnford is an emotional story about the struggle of two dogs and a cat, through the Canadian wilderness, to reach their owners.

■ Why did Atalanta agree to the footraces?

▲ An unrhymed Japanese poem, normally consisting of three lines of five, seven and five syllables

⬡ Choose the correct words. She (can hardly, can't hardly) lift the books.

● John Bunyan wrote this story about Christian and his journey to the Celestial City.

■ Who was the fastest runner in all of Greece?

▲ A sermon given to a congregation

⬡ Choose the antonym for *callous*. (emotional, veracity, deceitful)

● A fourteen-year-old girl searches for her mentally retarded brother in this story by Betsy Byars.

■ Why did Dionysus have Pythias arrested?

▲ The branch of linguistics which deals with the meanings of words

⬡ Choose the correct word. Did you select the fabric with a (coarse, course) texture for your pattern?

● This novel by John Steinbeck is about the Joads, Oklahoma farmers from the Dust Bowl region

■ What happened to anyone who ran a race against Atalanta and lost?

▲ Highly developed emotional and intellectual apprehension

⬡ Choose the antonym for *ineptitude*. (elastic, knack, weak)

● This story by Armstrong Sperry is about a son of a Polynesian chief who has overcome his fear of the sea so he can earn the respect of his people.

■ What was the condition King Dionysus made in order for Pythias to say his good-byes?

▲ Literary practice which stresses not objective reality as it is but rather the impressions the author or character derive from it.

⬡ Choose the correct word. (Bring, Take) extra blankets in your backpack.

● This book by Nina Bowden is about an adopted boy who runs away.

■ What did Hippomenes receive for winning the footrace against Atalanta?

▲ A document, such as the original manuscript of an author

⬡ Choose the correct word. A (continual, continuous) line of mourners greeted the widow.

● This author wrote *Emily of New Moon*, the first volume of a trilogy about a young girl's struggle to become a writer.

■ Who took Pythias' place while he went to say good-bye to his friends?

▲ An appeal in which a person asks for divine assistance at the beginning of a literary work

⬡ What does the prefix *non* mean?

Language Arts Trivial Pursuit

● *The Incredible Journey*

■ To keep her father quiet

▲ Haiku

⬡ Can hardly

Language Arts Trivial Pursuit

● George Orwell

■ Shooting it with arrows

▲ Science fiction

⬡ Adapted

Language Arts Trivial Pursuit

● *The Summer of the Swans*

■ He thought he planned to kill him.

▲ Semantics

⬡ Coarse

Language Arts Trivial Pursuit

● *Pilgrim's Progress*

■ Atalanta

▲ Homily

⬡ Emotional

Language Arts Trivial Pursuit

● *Call It Courage*

■ Someone took his place until he returned.

▲ Impressionism

⬡ Take

Language Arts Trivial Pursuit

● *The Grapes of the Wrath*

■ The person died

▲ Sensibility

⬡ Knack

Language Arts Trivial Pursuit

● Lucy Montgomery

■ Damon

▲ Invocation

⬡ Not

Language Arts Trivial Pursuit

● *The Finding*

■ Marriage to Atalanta

▲ Holograph

⬡ Continuous

● This author wrote *Human Comedy*, about a small town in the United States during World War II.

■ Who wished that everything he touched would turn to gold?

▲ A question asked to achieve a stylistic effect

⬡ Choose the correct word. She (implied, inferred) in her letter that she loved him.

● This author wrote the classic tale *Peter Pan*, about a trip to Never-Never Land.

■ What did Circe turn Ulysses' men into?

▲ A puzzle generally in the form of a question

⬡ What does the suffix *ish* mean?

● This author wrote *Homecoming*, about three abandoned children and their journey from Connecticut to Maryland.

■ Who granted King Midas his golden touch?

▲ Bitter, derisive expression whereby what is stated is the opposite of what is actually meant

⬡ Choose the correct word. If Gregory is ready, (then, than) we can leave now.

● This is a famous story by Tolkien, about the adventures of a creature who needs to find a treasure that is guarded by a dragon.

■ Who did Ulysses meet on his way to Circe's castle?

▲ A prose narrative involving a famous hero or the heroic exploits of kings and warriors

⬡ Choose the correct word. Her grandson always treated her (respectfully, respectively).

● This author wrote the well-known book *Watership Down* about a group of wild rabbits' search for a new home.

■ How did Ulysses' men escape the cave of the Cyclops?

▲ Writers attempting to account for the sources of their ideas

⬡ Choose the correct word. His (past, passed) caught up with him.

● In this popular story by Esther Forbes, a boy is about to involve himself in events in Boston that lead to the beginning of the Revolutionary War.

■ What was guarding Circe's castle?

▲ A type of short play, often a farce, popular in fifteenth and sixteenth-century England

⬡ What does the suffix *ir* mean?

● This author wrote *Jonathan Livingston Seagull*, about a seagull's effort to learn to fly.

■ How did Ulysses' men blind the Cyclops?

▲ A separate thing added to something

⬡ What does the prefix *ante* mean?

● An Indian girl is stranded on an island for eighteen years in this book by Scott O'Dell.

■ What drew the men's interest in Circe's castle?

▲ Usually an essay that precedes a literary work

⬡ Choose the correct word. Why don't you (sit, set) down and have some coffee?

GA1384

Language Arts Trivial Pursuit
● James M. Barrie

■ Pigs

▲ Riddle

⬡ Characteristic of

Language Arts Trivial Pursuit
● William Saroyan

■ King Midas

▲ Rhetorical question

⬡ Implied

Language Arts Trivial Pursuit
● *The Hobbit*

■ Hermes

▲ Saga

⬡ Respectfully

Language Arts Trivial Pursuit
● Cynthia Voight

■ Dionysus

▲ Sarcasm

⬡ Then

Language Arts Trivial Pursuit
● *Johnny Tremain*

■ Odd-looking beasts

▲ Interlude

⬡ Having the character of

Language Arts Trivial Pursuit
● Richard Adams

■ By hanging from the underbellies of the sheep

▲ Inspiration

⬡ Past

Language Arts Trivial Pursuit
● *Island of the Blue Dolphins*

■ Beautiful singing

▲ Introduction

⬡ Sit

Language Arts Trivial Pursuit
● Richard Bach

■ By poking a stick in his eye

▲ Adjunct

⬡ Before

● This collection of books by Jean de Brunhoff is about an elephant who leaves the jungle to live in Paris.

■ How long did Ulysses and his men stay with Circe?

▲ The part of a play preceding the climax

⬡ Spell the comparative form of the word *deadly*.

● This author wrote *My Friend Flicka*, about a filly owned and named by Ken McLaughlin.

■ Who gave Ulysses the wax to put into the ears of his men?

▲ The act of shortening a word, thought or group of words

⬡ Spell the superlative form of the word *flat*.

● This is the first of a series of books written by Madeleine L'Engle about Meg Murry, her small brother Charles and Calvin O'Keefe.

■ Why did Ulysses and his men come to Circe's island?

▲ A line of verse which continues into the following line without a grammatical break

⬡ Choose the correct word. (Can, May) we see you soon?

● This author wrote the well-known novel *For the Love of Benji*, which was based on the film about a dog involved in international intrigue.

■ True or False—Heroes in Greek mythology were largely or entirely mortal.

▲ A term of contempt given to speech or writing considered ugly sounding

⬡ Spell the comparative form of the word *good*.

● This tale is about an exchange of identity between the Prince of Wales and Tom Conty.

■ What did the Siren's song promise a person?

▲ The incidents which make up the plot of a play

⬡ Identify the adjective of comparison and then correct it. Steven has a bigger piece than anyone at the party.

● This author wrote *The Red Pony*, about a family in California.

■ In Greek mythology Aeolus was the keeper of the (waters, thunder, winds, rains).

▲ A figure of speech in which two unlike objects are compared

⬡ Spell the superlative form of the word *little*.

● This author wrote *Summer of the Monkeys*, about Jay and his dog spending the summer chasing monkeys.

■ What did the song of the siren promise Ulysses?

▲ Tales of love and chivalric adventure in both verse and prose

⬡ Choose the correct words. Who is the (more excitable, most excitable), you or Pete?

● This author wrote *Benji*, about the well-known dog and his adventures

■ When Aeolus gives Odysseus a bag of wind, what happens when his sailors open it by mistake?

▲ A critic praising a work of a friend or someone to whom he is obligated in hopes of receiving some favor in return

⬡ Spell the comparative form of the word *bad*.

Language Arts Trivial Pursuit

- ● Mary O'Hara
- ■ Circe
- ▲ Abbreviation
- ⬡ Flattest

Language Arts Trivial Pursuit

- ● Babar books
- ■ One year
- ▲ Rising action
- ⬡ Deadlier

Language Arts Trivial Pursuit

- ● I. Love
- ■ True
- ▲ Jargon
- ⬡ Better

Language Arts Trivial Pursuit

- ● *A Wrinkle in Time*
- ■ To rest
- ▲ Run-on line
- ⬡ May

Language Arts Trivial Pursuit

- ● John Steinbeck
- ■ Winds
- ▲ Metaphor
- ⬡ Least or littlest

Language Arts Trivial Pursuit

- ● *The Prince and the Pauper*
- ■ Whatever a person held most precious
- ▲ Intrigue
- ⬡ Biggest

Language Arts Trivial Pursuit

- ● Allison Thomas
- ■ He is blown off course.
- ▲ Puffery
- ⬡ Worse

Language Arts Trivial Pursuit

- ● Wilson Rawls
- ■ World's wisdom
- ▲ Romance
- ⬡ More excitable

44

GA1384

This author wrote *Little Lord Fauntleroy*, a classic book of a boy's home in New York to an earldom in England.

The Greeks prayed to him during plagues and in times of illness.

The principles governing the use of language for effective speaking and writing

Select the correct pronoun. The coach told all of the team members to take off (his or her, their) uniforms.

This novel by Arthur C. Clarke involves an adventure through an abyss of space to a planet on the farthest edge of the solar system on the *Discovery*.

Hebe became the wife of (Heracles, Apollo, Zeus, Hades).

Consists of sketches, dances and songs designed for amusement and frequently containing satirical comments on the personalities and events of the day

Select the correct pronoun. Debbie is better at math than (she, her).

This book is part of the series of The Chronicles of Narnia in which the captive Prince Rilion escapes from the Emerald Witch's underground kingdom.

For attempting to revive a dead man, Zeus killed Asclepius with a (monstrous snake, a thunderbolt, deadly disease, a stampede of horses).

A work expressing intense grief or mourning

Select the correct pronoun. One of the members cast (his or her, their) vote for me.

This is the first of two books about a Yorkshire veterinarian whose sense of humor prevails while he attends to the animals.

She was the goddess of witchcraft and black magic in Greek mythology.

A satirical attack on a person

Spell the plural of *Vietnamese*.

She wrote *Jacob Have I Loved*, about an older twin's lost birthright.

She was the goddess in Greek mythology who served nectar to the gods and goddesses on Mt. Olympus.

The fusion of music and drama

Select the correct pronoun. Most of the drivers turned (his or her, their) cars into the left lane.

This book by Jules Verne is about a journey down to the center of the earth.

Farmers, fishermen, athletes, statesmen and soldiers prayed to her for wealth and good fortune.

Having two or more possible meanings

Spell the plural of *waif*.

This story by Gary Paulsen is about a young boy's struggle to survive in a wilderness with only a hatchet.

The nectar Hebe served was believed to keep gods and goddesses (healthy, safe, youthful, wise).

A right-hand page in a book

Select the correct pronoun. Steven is as good a piano player as (he, him).

This author wrote *Sasha, My Friend*, about a wolf pup who helps Hallie get to know the wilderness in Montana.

The island of Rhodes was sacred to this Greek god and a famous statue of him stood there.

The editing or revising of a work for publication

Spell the plural of *fungus*.

Language Arts Trivial Pursuit

- ● *2001–A Space Odyssey*
- ■ Heracles
- ▲ Revue
- ⬡ She

Language Arts Trivial Pursuit

- ● Frances Hodgson Burnett
- ■ Asclepius
- ▲ Rhetoric
- ⬡ Their

Language Arts Trivial Pursuit

- ● *All Creatures Great and Small*
- ■ Hecate
- ▲ Lampoon
- ⬡ Vietnamese

Language Arts Trivial Pursuit

- ● *The Silver Chain*
- ■ Thunderbolt
- ▲ Lament
- ⬡ His or her

Language Arts Trivial Pursuit

- ● *Twenty Thousand Leagues Under the Sea*
- ■ Hecate
- ▲ Ambiguous
- ⬡ Waifs

Language Arts Trivial Pursuit

- ● Katherine Paterson
- ■ Hebe
- ▲ Melodrama
- ⬡ Their

Language Arts Trivial Pursuit

- ● Barbara Corcoran
- ■ Helios
- ▲ Redaction
- ⬡ Fungi

Language Arts Trivial Pursuit

- ● *Hatchet*
- ■ Youthful
- ▲ Recto
- ⬡ He

GA1384

● This author wrote *Man of War* and many other stories about horses.

■ He was one of the only Greek gods that was lame and deformed.

▲ The left-hand page or the back of a leaf

⬡ Spell the plural of *hypnosis*.

● This author wrote *Lassie Come Home*, about a faithful collie's journey through Great Britain.

■ He had the power to lull to sleep even the mightiest gods.

▲ The scientific study of language

⬡ Identify the verb and tell whether it is an action or linking word. These flowers grow quickly in the spring.

● This author wrote *Old Yeller*, about Travis and his dog trying to survive a summer in Texas.

■ This Greek god created many masterpieces in metal, including the golden throne of Zeus.

▲ A song designed for several voices

⬡ Spell the plural of *alumnus.*

● This story, by Louisa May Alcott, is about orphaned Rose Campbell who goes to live at Aunt Hill with six aunts and seven boy cousins.

■ He killed Patroclus during one of the last battles of the Trojan War.

▲ A poem sung to the accompaniment of a lyre

⬡ Identify the verb and tell whether it is an action or linking word. The trees are green again.

● This author wrote *Brighty of the Grand Canyon*, about a burro who helps to find an old man's murderer.

■ The marriage of Hephaestus and this goddess symbolized the union of art and beauty.

▲ A type of light verse

⬡ Spell the plural of *reef.*

● This story by Trina Paulus is an inspirational tale about a caterpillar who talks her way through the scary process of becoming a butterfly.

■ After killing Hector, he dragged his body around the walls of Troy for several days.

▲ An account of a person's life and experiences written by himself/herself

⬡ Identify the verbs and indicate which word is the helper. The birds are singing loudly this morning.

● This author wrote *Big Red* and two sequels about the champion Irish Setter.

■ He had hundreds of sons called the Dreams.

▲ Any repeated element in a poem

⬡ Identify the verb and tell whether it is an action or linking word. This dog has very good hearing.

● This tender story by Marjorie Kinnan Rawlings is about a relationship between a young boy and his tame fawn.

■ She blinded Polymestor, killed the children and was later transformed into a fiery-eyed dog.

▲ Nondramatic verse which tells a story

⬡ Identify what part of speech the italicized word is. The cards are on the table, *and* we are ready to play.

GA1384

● Eric Knight

■ Hypnos

▲ Linguistics

⬡ Grow, action

● Walter Farley

■ Hephaestus

▲ Verso

⬡ Hypnoses

● *Eight Cousins on the Aunt Hill*

■ Hector

▲ Lyric

⬡ Are, linking

● Fred Gipson

■ Hephaestus

▲ Madrigal

⬡ Alumni

● *Hope for the Flowers*

■ Achilles

▲ Memoir

⬡ Are, singing; *are* is the helper.

● Marguerite Henry

■ Aphrodite

▲ Limerick

⬡ Reefs

● *The Yearling*

■ Hecuba

▲ Narrative verse

⬡ Conjunction

● James Kjelgaard

■ Hypnos

▲ Repetend

⬡ Has, action

● This book, by Samuel L. Clemens, tells of his own experiences and observations of the West.

■ He was a Trojan priest who warned his people against taking the wooden horse inside the city.

▲ The point from which a story is seen or told

⬡ Identify what part of speech the italicized word is. The cacti *in* the desert are in bloom.

● This author wrote a collection of short stories, "Masterpieces of Adventure" being one of them.

■ After eating the food from this place, Odysseus' men forgot their homeland and wanted to stay where they were.

▲ A work, argumentative in nature, presenting a writer's viewpoint on a particular topic

⬡ Pick the best synonym for *garish*. (plain, precise, flashy)

● *Kidnapped* was written by this talented author who is famous for his ability to capture the fancy of many readers.

■ Laocoön and his sons were crushed to death by (a stampede, two sea serpents, the wooden horse).

▲ A short popular saying, generally an observation or a piece of advice

⬡ Choose the word that best completes this sentence. A _?_ smell came from the plugged up sink. (tantalizing, horrible, pleasant)

● This author wrote *The Black Pearl,* about a boy who gets powerful enemies when he finds a valuable pearl.

■ After being advised of the treachery going on in his palace, Odysseus goes home disguised as a (priest, sea nymph, beggar).

▲ This term now refers to the most important character in a play.

⬡ Pick the synonym for *fickle*. (deceitful, able, hostile)

● *The Old Man and the Sea*, about a Cuban fisherman and his battle with a great marlin, was written by this famous author.

■ It consists of twenty-four books and describes Odysseus' journey home after fighting for Greece against the city of Troy.

▲ A type of short comedy where the actors often wore masks and indulged in slapstick

⬡ Pick the best antonym for *pliant*. (slippery, limp, rigid)

● This well-known author wrote *The Tell-Tale Heart* and many other books of horror and surprise endings.

■ The music of his voice and lyre were so beautiful that animals, trees and stones followed him.

▲ A wandering poet or musician

⬡ Pick the antonym for *fierce*. (gentle, violent, intense)

● This author wrote *Trouble on Planet Earth* and about 140 other books in the Choose-Your-Own-Adventure Series.

■ The *Odyssey* begins on this island where Odysseus has been prisoner of the sea nymph Calypso for seven years.

▲ A theatrical form mingling song and spoken dialogue

⬡ Pick the best antonym for *prone*. (erect, sensitive, inclined)

● This author wrote *Avalanche* and *Two for Survival*, tales of survival of serious disasters.

■ This is a shrine where people consulted special priests or priestesses.

▲ A theme or character which recurs in literature or folklore

⬡ Pick the synonym for *gnash*. (sharp, close, grind)

GA1384

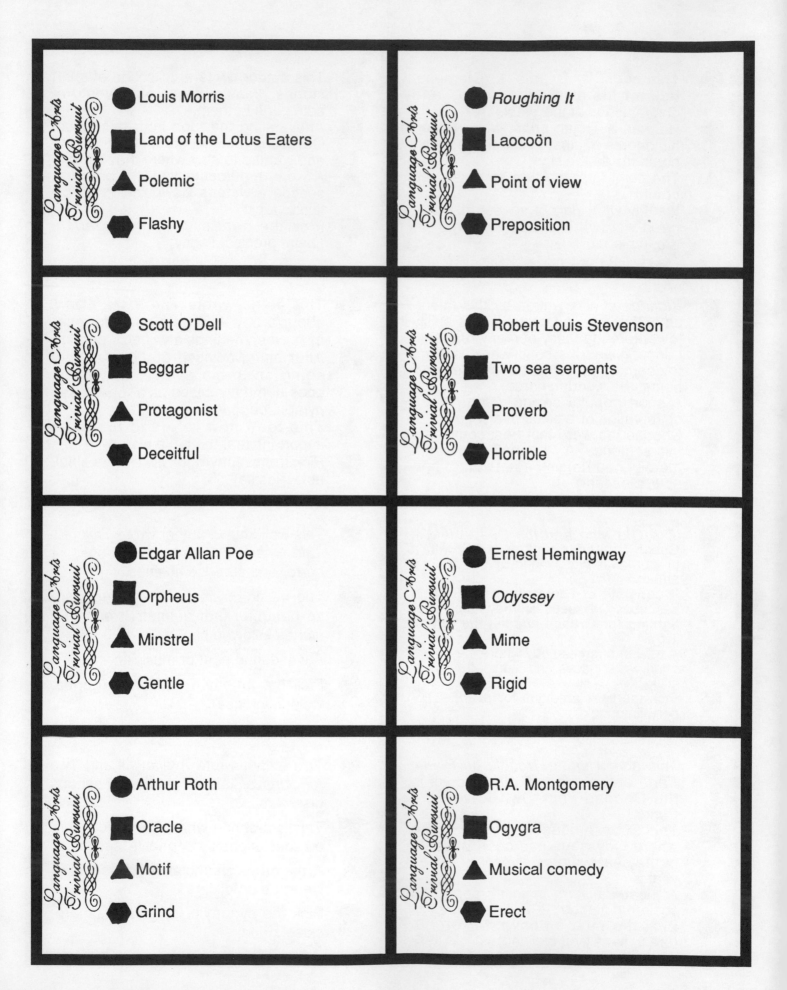

Language Arts Trivial Pursuit

● Louis Morris
■ Land of the Lotus Eaters
▲ Polemic
⬡ Flashy

Language Arts Trivial Pursuit

● *Roughing It*
■ Laocoön
▲ Point of view
⬡ Preposition

Language Arts Trivial Pursuit

● Scott O'Dell
■ Beggar
▲ Protagonist
⬡ Deceitful

Language Arts Trivial Pursuit

● Robert Louis Stevenson
■ Two sea serpents
▲ Proverb
⬡ Horrible

Language Arts Trivial Pursuit

● Edgar Allan Poe
■ Orpheus
▲ Minstrel
⬡ Gentle

Language Arts Trivial Pursuit

● Ernest Hemingway
■ *Odyssey*
▲ Mime
⬡ Rigid

Language Arts Trivial Pursuit

● Arthur Roth
■ Oracle
▲ Motif
⬡ Grind

Language Arts Trivial Pursuit

● R.A. Montgomery
■ Ogygra
▲ Musical comedy
⬡ Erect

GA1384

- This author wrote *The Strange Case of Dr. Jekyll and Mr. Hyde*, a classic horror story.
- He was the husband of Helen of Troy.
- A literary work produced for the purpose of providing the author with money
- Pick the synonym for *horrific*. (disagreeable, repulsive, inspired)

- Sara Creive, a gifted, well-mannered child, is one of the main characters in this book written by Frances Hodgson Burnett.
- She turned Scylla into a sea monster, part woman and part fish, with heads of dogs growing out of her waist.
- A literary expression not marked by rhyme or by metrical regularity
- Choose the synonym for *subtle*. (open, honest, crafty)

- This very famous tale is written by Herman Melville. It is about a great white whale and the men who hunted him.
- Before Odysseus went to fight in the Trojan War, he made this person the guardian of his son, Telemachus.
- The theory of versification, dealing with such matters as meter, rhyme, stanzaic patterns
- Pick the antonym for *inclusion*. (contain, separate, embrace)

- This is one book of The Lord of the Rings series by J.R.R. Tolkien. It is concerned with Hobbits.
- He lived on the island of Aeolia, which he surrounded with a brass wall so that no stranger could come to interfere with his duties.
- A preamble of introduction, especially to a speech
- Pick the correct word for the sentence. The (desert, dessert) is very dry and hot in the summertime.

- Kino, driven by the desire to give his wife and child what they deserved in life, was the main character of this famous book written by John Steinbeck.
- A fabled bird in Greek mythology that was always male and lived exactly 500 years; only one existed at a time.
- A dramatic presentation featuring only one character
- Choose the synonym for *sequel*. (appendage, before, advance)

- This is the second book of The Lord of the Rings series by J.R.R. Tolkien. It tells how the members fared after the breaking up of their fellowship.
- Its smoky crater was used as a workshop by Hephaestus. He stoked its fires to temper the thunderbolts he forged for Zeus.
- A fictional prose narrative of extreme length
- Pick the correct word for the sentence. The (steel, steal) rod fell when the lightning hit.

- This story, by Marguerite Henry, is of a young girl who almost singlehandedly saves the wild mustang from extinction.
- Glaucus fell in love with her when he saw her walking on the shore by the Strait of Messina.
- A long essay on a subject of scholarly nature
- Choose the antonym for *timid*. (confident, weak, cowardly)

- This author wrote *Winter of the White Seal* about a young Englishman who is marooned on an island in Antarctica.
- This was the magical goatskin which Zeus used to cover his shield.
- The use of words whose sounds seem to express or reinforce their meanings
- Pick out the verb phrase. She had been frying hamburgers for a very long time.

GA1384

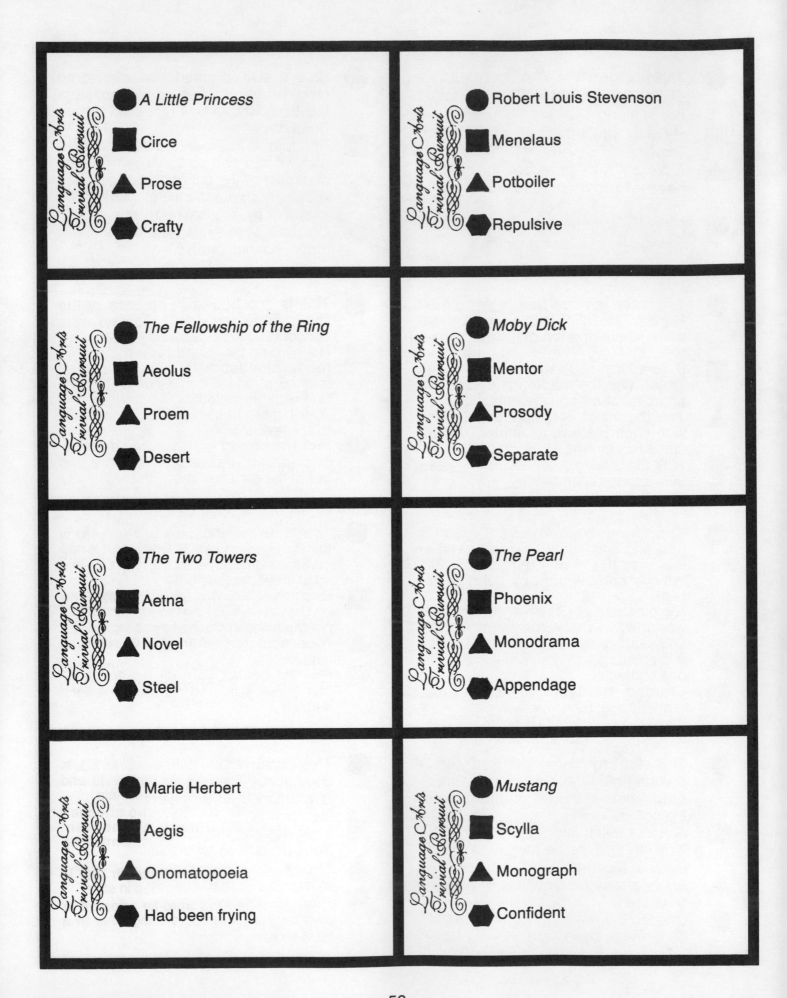

Language Arts Trivial Pursuit

- ● *A Little Princess*
- ■ Circe
- ▲ Prose
- ⬡ Crafty

Language Arts Trivial Pursuit

- ● Robert Louis Stevenson
- ■ Menelaus
- ▲ Potboiler
- ⬡ Repulsive

Language Arts Trivial Pursuit

- ● *The Fellowship of the Ring*
- ■ Aeolus
- ▲ Proem
- ⬡ Desert

Language Arts Trivial Pursuit

- ● *Moby Dick*
- ■ Mentor
- ▲ Prosody
- ⬡ Separate

Language Arts Trivial Pursuit

- ● *The Two Towers*
- ■ Aetna
- ▲ Novel
- ⬡ Steel

Language Arts Trivial Pursuit

- ● *The Pearl*
- ■ Phoenix
- ▲ Monodrama
- ⬡ Appendage

Language Arts Trivial Pursuit

- ● Marie Herbert
- ■ Aegis
- ▲ Onomatopoeia
- ⬡ Had been frying

Language Arts Trivial Pursuit

- ● *Mustang*
- ■ Scylla
- ▲ Monograph
- ⬡ Confident

● This author wrote *The Outsiders* and other books about gang warfare.

■ A she-goat whose milk nourished the infant Zeus on the slope of Crete's M. Ida

▲ An arrangement of important ideas in similar grammatical construction; often reinforced by verbal echoes

⬡ Identify the compound predicate. The clown twisted and jumped around the arena.

● This author wrote *The Sea-Wolf*, an adventure on the high seas with Captain Wolf Larson.

■ These gentle radiant daughters of Zeus and Eurynome went about among mankind spreading joy and peace.

▲ The restatement in different words of the sense of a piece of work

⬡ Pick out all the adjectives in this sentence. The tiny needle fell onto the thick, dirty carpet.

● This author wrote *Shivering Sands* and many other gothics involving romance and adventure.

■ He was a tall tree and son of Mother Earth. Heracles lifted the giant from Earth and held him there until he strangled.

▲ A term sometimes limited to the drama, designating the point in a story at which the writer begins his/her action

⬡ Identify the subject of this sentence: Will you recognize my house?

● This third book in the The Lord of the Rings series, written by J.R.R. Tolkien, tells of the opposing strategies of Gandalf and Sauron.

■ Annual rites performed by worshippers of Demeter, goddess of the harvest

▲ An expansion of an idea

⬡ Pick out the demonstrative pronoun. Those are my earrings in the bottom of the pool.

● This author wrote *White Dawn* and *Frozen Fire*, tales of great courage taking place in the Arctic regions of our country.

■ Three hell-hags with brass wings and brass claws who pounced upon those who offended the gods and tortured them forever

▲ A volume of works, usually reprints, by an author or on related subjects

⬡ Name the subject of this sentence: Has anyone seen a black and white collie recently?

● This book by C.S. Lewis tells how King Caspian sailed through magic waters to the end of the world.

■ The part of Tartarus which was the abode of the blessed

▲ Refers to either meter, feet or verse

⬡ Tell whether the italicized pronoun is interrogative or demonstrative. *Which* of my books do you want?

● This author wrote *Arm of the Starfish*, about Adam Eddington's summer with a marine biologist.

■ A Libyan shepherd who found a ring which allowed him to become invisible at will

▲ A brief prose tale

⬡ Name the subject of this sentence: Write your name on the paper.

● *The Magician's Nephew*, by C.S. Lewis, is about how Aslan created this place and gave the gift of speech to its animals.

■ A host of small demons who attended Hecate, queen of hags, as she went about her rounds in Tartarus, tormenting the shades

▲ A lyric or poem of some length that is serious in subject and dignified in style

⬡ Identify the italicized word as adjective or pronoun. *All* oceans are dangerous in a storm.

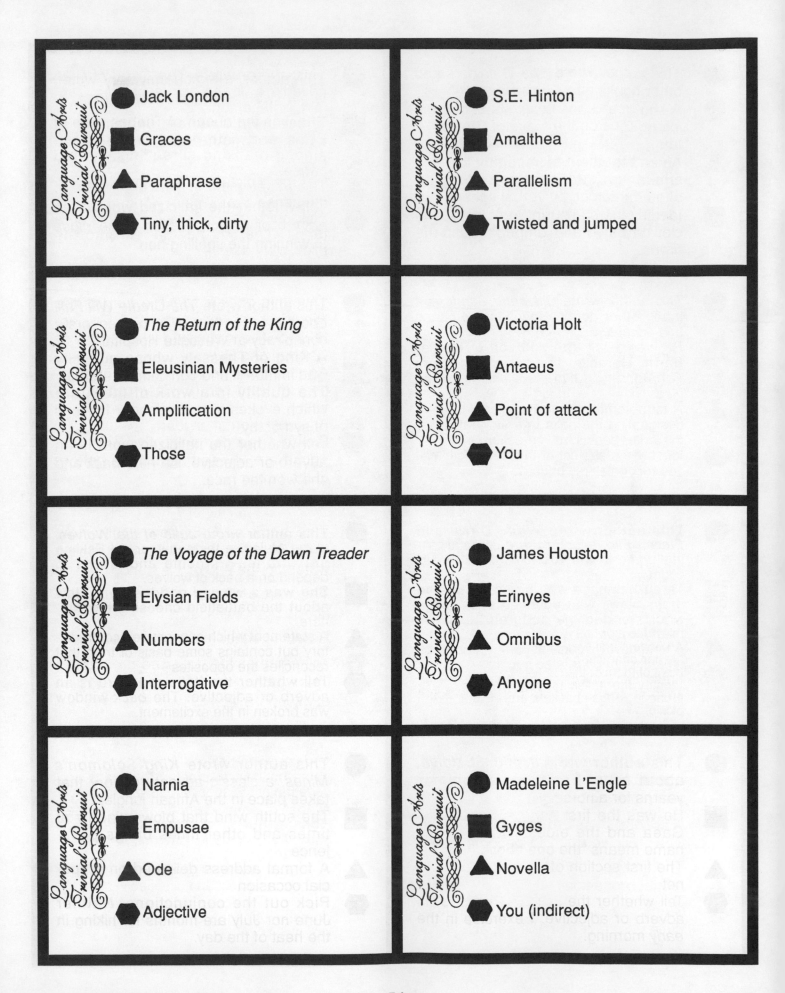

Language Arts Trivial Pursuit

- ● Jack London
- ■ Graces
- ▲ Paraphrase
- ⬡ Tiny, thick, dirty

Language Arts Trivial Pursuit

- ● S.E. Hinton
- ■ Amalthea
- ▲ Parallelism
- ⬡ Twisted and jumped

Language Arts Trivial Pursuit

- ● *The Return of the King*
- ■ Eleusinian Mysteries
- ▲ Amplification
- ⬡ Those

Language Arts Trivial Pursuit

- ● Victoria Holt
- ■ Antaeus
- ▲ Point of attack
- ⬡ You

Language Arts Trivial Pursuit

- ● *The Voyage of the Dawn Treader*
- ■ Elysian Fields
- ▲ Numbers
- ⬡ Interrogative

Language Arts Trivial Pursuit

- ● James Houston
- ■ Erinyes
- ▲ Omnibus
- ⬡ Anyone

Language Arts Trivial Pursuit

- ● Narnia
- ■ Empusae
- ▲ Ode
- ⬡ Adjective

Language Arts Trivial Pursuit

- ● Madeleine L'Engle
- ■ Gyges
- ▲ Novella
- ⬡ You (indirect)

This book, written by C.S. Lewis, has the same name as the main character who, with his army, conquers the Telmarines.

A beautiful youth for whom Artemis broke her vows of maidenhood

The process of separating a subject into its parts

Identify the italicized word as adjective or pronoun. *Some* bought popcorn while watching the game.

This author, a famous mystery writer, wrote *Witness for the Prosecution*.

She was the queen of Thebes, wife of Laius and mother and wife of Oedipus.

To form a picture in the mind

Tell whether the italicized word is an adverb or adjective. She came *close* to winning the spelling bee.

This book, by C.S. Lewis, deals with how evil came to Narnia and how Aslan led his people to a new paradise.

She is the goddess of the dawn.

A line of five metrical feet

Identify the italicized word as adjective or pronoun. *Most* are welcomed personally by the host.

This author wrote *The Cradle Will Fall*, about a young lawyer who uncovers a conspiracy at Westlake Hospital.

A King of Thessaly whose audacity was immortal and punishment eternal

The quality in a work of literature which evokes from the reader feelings of sympathy

Tell whether the italicized word is an adverb or adjective. He held *back* and she won the race.

This is the author of a series of books called *The Dark Is Rising* and *Silver on the Tree*. One of the books is about Will and Bran being taken to the haunting timeless Lost Land to find the crystal sword that can vanquish the dark.

This huge, savage beast roamed the slopes of Mt. Erymanthus in Arcadia, making life a misery to all who lived there.

An impersonal way for an author to present his/her characters without an obvious judgment of them or their actions

Identify the italicized word as adjective or pronoun. *Those* baskets are for the Easter picnic.

This author wrote *Julie of the Wolves*, about Mujax, a thirteen-year-old Eskimo girl who leaves home and learns to depend on a pack of wolves.

She was a winged goddess who flew about the battlefield choosing the winners.

A statement which appears self-contradictory but contains some basis of truth that reconciles the opposites

Tell whether the italicized word is an adverb or adjective. The *back* window was broken in the excitement.

This author wrote *National Velvet* about a butcher's daughter who yearns for a horse.

He was the first son of Uranus and Gaea and the eldest Titan, whose name means "the one above."

The first section of a Petrarchan sonnet

Tell whether the italicized word is an adverb or adjective. I exercise in the *early* morning.

This author wrote *King Solomon's Mines*, a classic adventure story that takes place in the African jungle.

The south wind that blows warmly at times and other times brings pestilence

A formal address delivered on a special occasion

Pick out the conjunctions. Neither June nor July are months for hiking in the heat of the day.

55

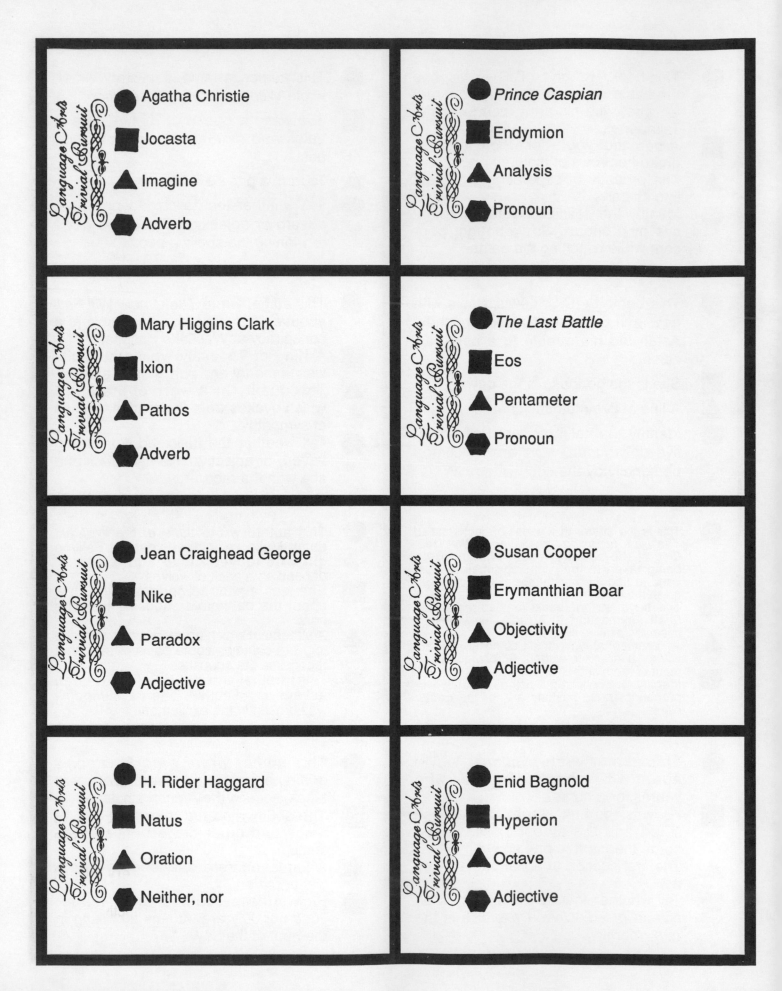

Language Arts Trivial Pursuit

- ● Agatha Christie
- ■ Jocasta
- ▲ Imagine
- ⬡ Adverb

Language Arts Trivial Pursuit

- ● *Prince Caspian*
- ■ Endymion
- ▲ Analysis
- ⬡ Pronoun

Language Arts Trivial Pursuit

- ● Mary Higgins Clark
- ■ Ixion
- ▲ Pathos
- ⬡ Adverb

Language Arts Trivial Pursuit

- ● *The Last Battle*
- ■ Eos
- ▲ Pentameter
- ⬡ Pronoun

Language Arts Trivial Pursuit

- ● Jean Craighead George
- ■ Nike
- ▲ Paradox
- ⬡ Adjective

Language Arts Trivial Pursuit

- ● Susan Cooper
- ■ Erymanthian Boar
- ▲ Objectivity
- ⬡ Adjective

Language Arts Trivial Pursuit

- ● H. Rider Haggard
- ■ Natus
- ▲ Oration
- ⬡ Neither, nor

Language Arts Trivial Pursuit

- ● Enid Bagnold
- ■ Hyperion
- ▲ Octave
- ⬡ Adjective

GA1384

● Susan Cooper wrote this book about the dangerous and mysterious events that led to the discovery of the stolen grail. This dreadful and vengeful power is called from the ocean's depths.

■ The eldest Titan who married his sister, Lethys, who bore three thousand daughters, the Oceanids

▲ A short, simple story illustrating a moral lesson

⬡ Pick out the conjunction. Pete or Sam will play checkers with you.

● These two boys are the main characters of a series of books written by Frankie D. Dixon.

■ A spring sacred to the Muses, formed when their flying horse, Pegasus, struck the ground with his hoof

▲ A poem in which the writer recants a statement made in a previous poem

⬡ Pick out the predicate nominative. Lassie is a popular TV personality.

● This book by Frank Herbert is about a planet of harsh deserts where water was rare and huge sandworms caused fear in the hearts of people.

■ She was the dark-robed goddess of light and daughter of Chaos.

▲ Any song, hymn of joy, praise or triumph

⬡ Pick out the preposition. Are you going to look at the sunset?

● This author wrote five outstanding nature books for children, *Water Shy* being one of them.

■ She was queen of Ithaca and model wife of mythology.

▲ A word, sentence or verse which reads the same either backward or forward.

⬡ Pick out the two predicate nominatives. The essential items for Ping-Pong are the paddles and net.

● This author wrote the book *The Runaway Robot* about a robot's travel through space.

■ Queen of Lydia whom Heracles was condemned to serve as a slave to expiate the murder of Iphitus

▲ A piece of writing or a formal speech praising someone

⬡ Pick out the preposition. The dog has been barking for a long time.

● This author wrote a series of books titled Amazing Indian Children. *Keener* is one of these books.

■ The seven daughters of Atlas who became a constellation after their deaths

▲ An ancient drawing or inscription on a wall or other surface

⬡ Pick out the predicate nominative. Television is a favorite pastime for many people.

● She is the main character in a series of mysteries, *The Gatehouse Mystery* and *Mystery on the Mississippi* being among them.

■ He was taught vine culture by his father. He was king of Chios and had a comely daughter named Merope.

▲ A movable stage upon which the medieval mystery plays were presented. It is also an outdoor performance.

⬡ Pick out the predicate nominative. Julie is the captain of the team.

● This story by Shel Silverstein is about a tree that gives and gives until it has nothing left.

■ The enormous serpent sent by Hero to Harry Leto from one end of the earth to the other

▲ An atmosphere of mystery about something or somebody

⬡ Pick out the predicate adjective. The movie was scary!

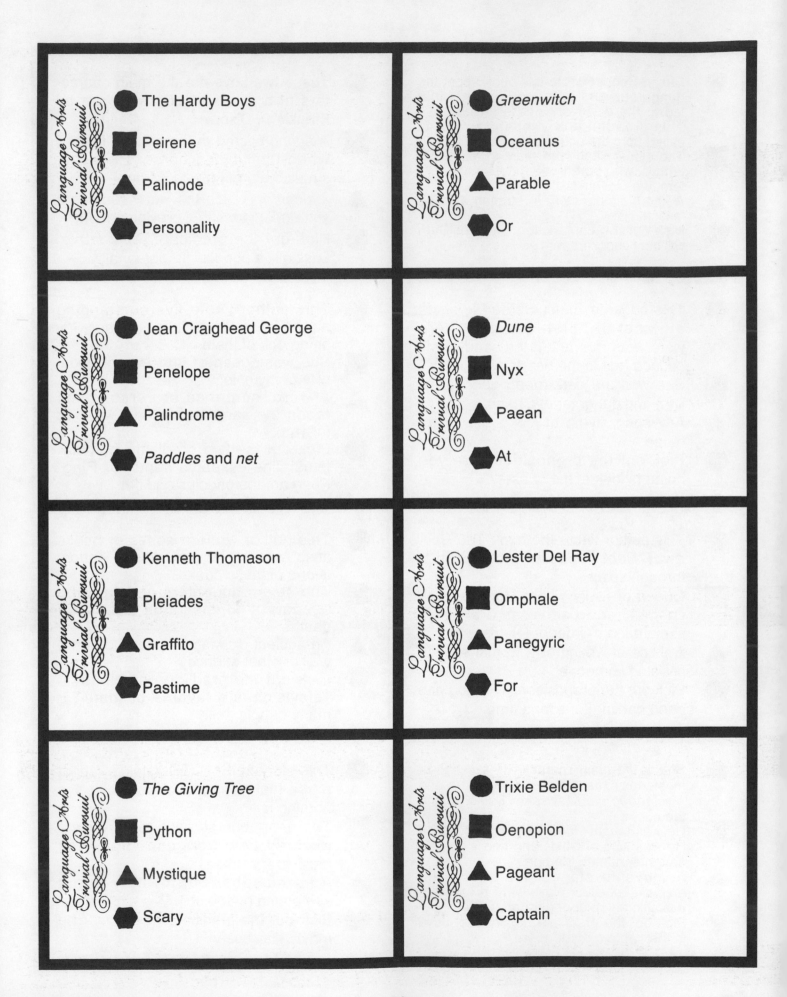

Language Arts Trivial Pursuit

- ● The Hardy Boys
- ■ Peirene
- ▲ Palinode
- ⬡ Personality

Language Arts Trivial Pursuit

- ● *Greenwitch*
- ■ Oceanus
- ▲ Parable
- ⬡ Or

Language Arts Trivial Pursuit

- ● Jean Craighead George
- ■ Penelope
- ▲ Palindrome
- ⬡ *Paddles* and *net*

Language Arts Trivial Pursuit

- ● *Dune*
- ■ Nyx
- ▲ Paean
- ⬡ At

Language Arts Trivial Pursuit

- ● Kenneth Thomason
- ■ Pleiades
- ▲ Graffito
- ⬡ Pastime

Language Arts Trivial Pursuit

- ● Lester Del Ray
- ■ Omphale
- ▲ Panegyric
- ⬡ For

Language Arts Trivial Pursuit

- ● *The Giving Tree*
- ■ Python
- ▲ Mystique
- ⬡ Scary

Language Arts Trivial Pursuit

- ● Trixie Belden
- ■ Oenopion
- ▲ Pageant
- ⬡ Captain

The Growing Family of Good 🍎 Apple Products and Services Includes:

4 Periodicals to Meet the Needs of Educators

THE GOOD APPLE NEWSPAPER Here's a year's supply of creative, easy-to-use ideas for your classroom. Each issue contains 16 BIG (17 1/2" x 22 1/2") pages and is filled with a limitless supply of ideas for all areas of the curriculum. Designed to provide you with a wealth of valuable materials. Packed with seasonal activities, arts and crafts, contests, bulletin boards and unique units of study— all designed by teachers. For teachers grades 2-8.

LOLLIPOPS Help make those early developmental years LEARNING YEARS with Good Apple's #1 resource for early childhood education. Provides timely teaching tips that will make your classroom come alive and articles that help to create a successful environment. Enjoy eye-catching bulletin boards, cut-and-paste activities, craft projects, songs, finger plays, gameboards, calendars and more. For preschool-grade 2 teachers.

CHALLENGE **Challenge** yourself and your students to inspiring interviews, thought-provoking games and activities, complete units of study and pages from our 20-page reproducible section. This wealth of articles, interviews, activities and units with special emphasis on art, music, drama, literature and the sciences will provide a special **Challenge** for your gifted students. For teachers and parents of gifted children preschool-grade 8.

OASIS Thousands of teachers are continuing to choose **Oasis** as their middle school classroom resource. Isn't it refreshing to know there's an **Oasis** of new and exciting ideas especially for middle grade teachers! It features interdisciplinary units, 2 full-color posters, current articles of interest, calendars, biographies, etc. For middle grade teachers 5-9.

Good Apple Idea and Activity Books

In all subject areas for all grade levels, preschool-grade 8+. Idea books, activity books, bulletin board books, units of instruction, reading, creativity, readiness, gameboards, science, math, social studies, responsibility education, self-concept, gifted, seasonal ideas, arts/crafts, poetry, language arts and teacher helpers.

Activity Posters • Note Pads • Software • Videos

and there is still more!

Good Apple is also proud to distribute Monday Morning books. This fine line of educational products includes creativity, arts and crafts, reading, language arts and early learning resources.

If a school supply store is not available in your area, please write for a FREE catalog to GOOD APPLE, 1204 Buchanan St., Box 299, Carthage, IL 62321-0299.

Language Arts Trivial Pursuit (Junior High Level)

Language Arts Trivial Pursuit Book/Game Series is created for students as a fun way to teach and reinforce language arts concepts. Each of the books in the series is written to develop basic skills, increase understanding of literary terms and increase knowledge of popular books and authors. For grades 7-9.

Meet the Author

Mary Anne McElmurry has been a teacher for twenty-five years with junior high students. As a teacher at Kino Learning Center, Inc., Tucson, Arizona, she has worked in the areas of values development and language arts. Mary Anne has authored many of the Good Apple values series.

Other Books in the Trivial Pursuit Series:

GA1072 Math Trivial Pursuit (Primary)
GA1073 Math Trivial Pursuit (Intermediate)
GA1074 Math Trivial Pursuit (Junior High)

GA1385 Science Trivial Pursuit (Primary)
GA1386 Science Trivial Pursuit (Intermediate)
GA1387 Science Trivial Pursuit (Junior High)

Finished box:

Filled box:

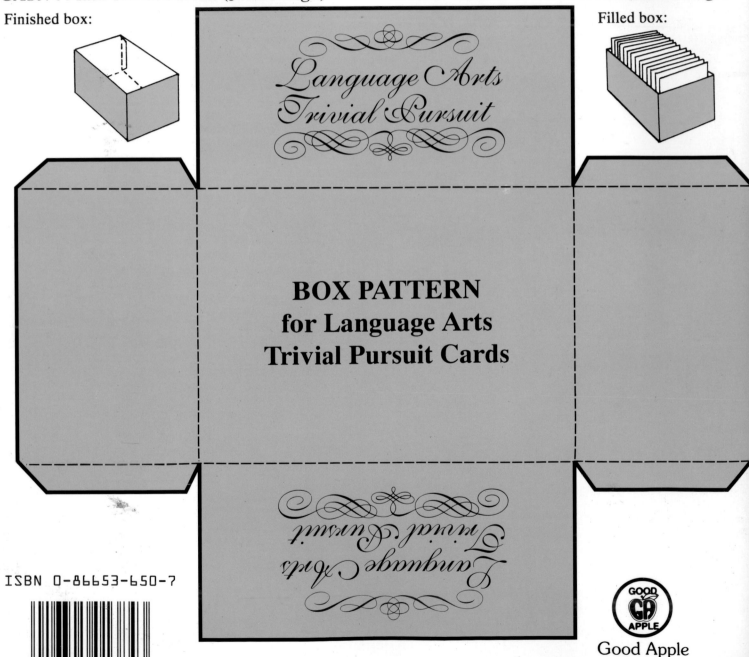

Language Arts Trivial Pursuit

**BOX PATTERN
for Language Arts
Trivial Pursuit Cards**

ISBN 0-86653-650-7

0 16305 01384 3

Good Apple
1204 Buchanan St., Box 299
Carthage, IL 62321-0299